Needlepoint

Designs from Amish Quilts

Laura Siegel Gilberg and
Barbara Ballinger Buchholz

Charles Scribner's Sons   New York

746.44
B

We dedicate this book to the Amish who stitched these quilts, and to our husbands—Maxwell Gilberg and Edward J. Buchholz—and our families who encouraged us throughout this project.

page 32: From *Home Life in Colonial Days* by Alice Morse Earle, Stockbridge, Mass.: The Berkshire Traveller Press, 1974.

page 49: "A Blessing of Women" copyright 1974, 1975 by Stanley Kunitz and reprinted by permission of the author.

Library of Congress Cataloging in Publication Data

Buchholz, Barbara.
   Needlepoint designs from Amish quilts.

   "A House and garden book."
   Bibliography: p. 142
   1. Canvas embroidery—Patterns. 2. Coverlets, Amish. I. Gilberg, Laura, joint author. II. House & garden. III. Title.
TT778.C3B82   746.4'4   77-24600
ISBN 0-684-15070-0

1 3 5 7 9 11 13 15 17 19 MD/C 20 18 16 14 12 10 8 6 4 2

Printed in the United States of America

Acknowledgments

There are many people we would like to thank for helping with this book.

We thank our collector friends who never grew impatient as we pored over their treasures: Phyllis Haders, Jonathan and Gail Holstein, Joel and Kate Kopp, George E. Schoellkopf.

We thank craftswoman Cheryl Youngman for working out the mathematical calculations for the graphs and for designing the outlines and stitch diagrams, and artist Sherry Lifson for drawing the graphs.

We thank our diligent group of needlepointers: Estelle Ballinger, Mae Berger, Susan Blumstein, Sylvia Brody, Elaine Chubb, Beverly Enright, Edna Fernandez, Judith Gross, Lawrence Hoffman, Florence Horn, Gloria Hutter, Ann Light, Lilian Lowy, Phyllis Margulies, Sandy Owens, Lilly Reisman, Sandra Richner, Jean Sedita, Myrtle Silverstadt, Pat Wilkins.

We thank our photographers: Robert Brandau for taking the color photographs of the stitched canvases in varied settings, including the Amish countryside, and for his photographs of the Amish; and Robert Gilberg for close-up photographs of the stitches for our instruction pages.

We thank the House & Garden Guides staff for their assistance, especially Louis O. Gropp for giving us a chance to develop our original designs and for his welcome suggestions; Elaine Greene Weisburg for her valuable ideas and for helping to prepare the manuscript; Albert T. Hamowy for the long hours he spent designing the book and for his unfailing good humor while doing it; Carol Knobloch for her creative assistance to Al Hamowy; Paul H. Bonner, Jr., of the Book Division of The Condé Nast Publications, and Elinor Parker of Charles Scribner's Sons, for their warm support.

We thank many other people: America Hurrah Antiques for lending us quilts and photographs of quilts; Alan H. Ballinger for photographing many of the quilts so that we could make up the graphs and outlines; Jo Bucher of American Crewel and Canvas Studio for the use of the raised stitch and princess stitch from her book, *Complete Guide to Creative Needlepoint*; Jerry Fales and Donnë Florence for editing suggestions; Ann Freedman for photographing the Kenneth Noland painting; Galerie Denise René for the photograph of the Victor Vasarely painting; collector Rhea Goodman; Mr. and Mrs. Benuel S. King for the use of their Amish farm for many of the outdoor photographs; collector Sarah Melvin; the Metropolitan Museum of Art; authors-collectors Myron and Patsy Orlofsky; Olivier Rebbot for his fine photographs of Amish people on pages 6–7 and 20–21; Mrs. William Weimer III for letting us photograph her house and property in Churchtown, Pennsylvania.

Contents

3 Acknowledgments
6 Foreword
8 Introduction
10 The Amish and Their Quilts
20 Basics for Needlepointing Amish Designs
28 Stitch Glossary
32 Color Photographs of the Amish Designs
Instructions
50 1. Bars
52 2. Shadows
56 3. Sunshine and Shadow
58 4. Rainbow
60 5. Bars
62 6. Courthouse Steps
64 7. Bars
66 8. Diamond
68 9. Split Bars
70 10. Checkerboard
74 11. Single Irish Chain
76 12. Nine-Patch

80 13. Split Bars
82 14. Special Projects
92 15. Improved Nine-Patch
94 16. Variable Star
96 17. Diamond
98 18. Lone Star
102 19. Railroad Crossing
108 20. Log Cabin-Straight Furrow
110 21. Streak of Lightning
112 22. Baby's Block Variation
116 23. Stars and Stripes
120 24. Baskets or Cake Stand
122 25. Baskets or Cake Stand
124 26. Jake Mast

128 Additional Stitches
132 Alphabets
136 Monograms
140 Yarn Chart
142 Bibliography
143 Suppliers

An Amish woman returning home with a goose.

Foreword
by Joel Kopp

This book is tangible evidence of the widespread recognition of the Amish quilt as an important American design form. Now collected internationally by museums and individuals, Amish quilts were virtually unknown outside the Amish enclaves ten years ago. Of the dozen or so books then available on quilts and other country arts, not one illustrated or even mentioned this genre. I personally know of no major museum, other than the Pennsylvania Farm and Home Museum in Lancaster County, that then owned an Amish quilt. As dealers in American folk art, my wife and I shared in the exciting, meteoric rise in popularity of the Amish quilt.

In the late sixties, when we began to buy and sell quilts, we would occasionally see a worn, uninteresting Amish example in Pennsylvania. Amish quilts of real quality began to be sought only after the landmark 1971 show at the Whitney Museum in New York, where the Holstein collection of quilts was exhibited. That collection and the catalogue written by Jonathan Holstein presented quilts for the first time as serious graphic art. The quilts were shown as wall hangings, and the similarities between their geometric designs and contemporary nonobjective paintings became obvious.

Among other superb quilts in the Whitney show the Amish work stood out. Few visitors to the museum had ever seen anything like these simple, bold, modern-looking designs. Surprising combinations of vibrant and moody colors and unusually tight, precise quilting added an extra dimension to the beauty of the designs. The impact of the show mounted as it traveled to other museums, including the Louvre.

Several new books about quilts appeared at this time, both reflecting and broadening the international interest in old quilts of every kind: not only the graphic and Amish, but also appliqués, pieced country quilts, trapunto, and all-white examples.

Dealers scoured Pennsylvania. Many Amish families were willing to sell some of their old quilts, and at farm sales and auctions we began to see active bidding by dealers who had overlooked Amish quilts before. Although the Amish are still making quilts in their traditional patterns and with a high quality of needlework, it is the early quilts that have a special appeal: for their rarity, for the unique colors produced by hand-dyeing and natural materials, for the look and feel of the early woolen fabrics used. The avid collecting of the past six or seven years has taken almost all the early examples the Amish will part with. The demand now far exceeds the supply, and the prices reflect this.

Not all admirers of Amish quilts can be owners, and that is why I welcome this timely book. The excellent, authentic quilt examples searched out by crafts editor Barbara Buchholz and adapted for canvas needlework by craftswoman-teacher Laura Gilberg provide a wonderful way to enjoy and understand the unique design and color of Amish quilts without the effort and expense of acquiring one. The textures of the stitched pieces in this book bear a surprising similarity to the textures that are so remarkable in Amish quilting, and the wide range of yarn colors available today allows an accurate rendition of the Amish palette.

Quilt making was something of an entertainment for Amish women, who usually gathered in large groups to quilt their pieced tops. The workmanship was under the scrutiny of all who participated, and quality was expected. Quality was achieved, and quality can mark the needlework produced by those who use the carefully adapted designs in these pages.

Joel Kopp and his wife, Kate, are the owners of America Hurrah Antiques, a gallery and shop in New York City that specializes in quilts and other American folk art.

7

Introduction

How This Book Came to Be

Three years ago, frustrated by the scarcity and costliness of Amish quilts of the peak period (1870–1930) and longing to enjoy one in my home, I translated a favorite example into a 17-by-17$\frac{1}{2}$-inch needlepoint wall hanging (opposite top). It was a great success. The Amish geometry is easily adapted to canvas work, and the intense colors can be matched quite exactly. I quickly made another Amish quilt canvas and soon found myself preparing kits with marked canvases and the necessary yarns for avid friends.

I was satisfied that one could capture the composition and coloration of the quilts, yet there was no indication in my needlepoint of the actual quilting texture. Then I met a very talented craftswoman-teacher, Laura S. Gilberg, proprietor of The Nimble Thimble, a shop so filled with wonderful needlework supplies that my visits there made me feel like a child set loose in a toy store. Laura took my Amish quilt adaptations a step further, showing me how innumerable stitches for canvas work could simulate quilting.

We showed our new developments to my editor in chief at the House & Garden Guides, Louis O. Gropp, who is himself an enthusiastic needleworker, and he suggested an article on the subject. Out of this article our book grew.

Laura and I looked at hundreds of Amish quilts to find suitable projects for our book. We went to the city's museums, to folk art and antique shops, to collectors' homes. We talked with quilt experts, and we studied every book on quilts that contained Amish work. We chose our examples for their visual impact and their suitability for canvas needlework. Half the designs we selected are well known. The others are more unusual. One design (Rainbow) is not Amish but Pennsylvania Dutch, and it shows how a neighboring culture was influenced by the Amish designs. Some outstanding traditional patterns in this book are Bars in three different color combinations, Split Bars in two color variations, Diamonds with and without corners, Baskets in two color mixtures. Quilts that seemed to be one-of-a-kind pieces are Railroad Crossing (bold X forms enclosing tiny triangles in an endless rainbow of colors), Baby's Block Variation (a cascade of boxes in warm tones), and Lone Star (a brilliant large star fragmented into many colors and floating in a sea of navy blue).

To produce our instructions and diagrams, we took photographs of the quilts and enlarged them on a photostat machine as nearly as possible to 14 inches square, typical needlepoint pillow or wall hanging size. Laura and a student, Cheryl Youngman, drew an outline of each quilt pattern and worked out the stitches to be placed in each area to best simulate the quilting and create an interesting design.

Using a Craft Persian yarn chart, which provides a wide range of yarn colors, Laura and I matched the yarns with the original quilt fabrics. In almost all cases the color variance, if any, was negligible.

To show that the designs could work equally well with other yarns and threads, and in other projects besides pillows and hangings, we created a needlework of embroidery thread for a dollhouse, large wall hangings of rug yarn and pearl cotton #1, a latch-hooked rug, a picture in pearl cotton #3, and pillows of velvet yarns.

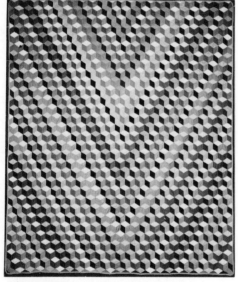

Baby's Blocks. Ohio, circa 1930.
(Courtesy of America Hurrah Antiques)

Victor Vasarely. *Hat A,* 1971.
(Courtesy of Galerie Denise René)

Split Bars in needlepoint.
Designed from a Pennsylvania
quilt, circa 1900.
(Courtesy of George E. Schoellkopf Gallery)

The Place of Amish Quilt Design in Today's World

Amish designs, whether in quilt or needlepoint form, are highly sophisticated, though based on a very simple format. Many people react similarly upon seeing either rendition for the first time. They are amazed that a people who are so conservative and inward-turning, so outside the mainstream, whose simple culture seems to be one of deprivation, could create such a sophisticated body of work. The quilts (and needlepoints) bear an unmistakable resemblance to contemporary art, and it would perhaps be easier to accept them if they had been inspired by a Kenneth Noland (below) or a Victor Vasarely (opposite below left). The fields of expressive color used in Amish quilts help to dispel the myth that their world was one of only blacks and grays, and their strong design sense and exquisite stitchery are testimony to the creativity all humans share.

For many years the decorative aspect of fundamental objects was overlooked. Quilts always prized for their fine craftsmanship, their usefulness, and their sentimental appeal were rarely viewed as fine art by critics because of their practical purpose. They were instead considered "folk art," functional objects that brightened their surroundings.

It is because of American collectors, craftspeople, and writers that a change in attitude took place. The display of pieced quilts as wall art in the Whitney Museum's 1971 show helped alter the notion that something functional could not be art. Subsequent shows, "12 Great Quilts from the American Wing" at the Metropolitan Museum of Art in 1974 and "The Flowering of American Folk Art" at the Whitney Museum in the same year, gave the public more opportunity to see quilts as art instead of bedcovers.

This renewed interest in quilts was not limited to museum shows. Quilters' cooperatives, church gatherings, and women's sewing circles began to proliferate once again across the country, with members busily copying old familiar patterns and inventing new ones. More and more regional fairs exhibit quilts and award prizes to the most worthy examples. Some antique and folk art galleries now deal exclusively in quilts. Magazines and books devote articles or chapters or even their entire contents to quilts: history, techniques, uses in rooms. Experts can be found teaching classes in quilt making. Reproductions of quilts appear on calendars, greeting cards, fabrics. Thus the interest in an important American tradition is kept alive.

This book is an outgrowth of the renewed interest in quilts. It is also an outgrowth of what many people call the great crafts revival of the 1970s. More people than ever want to add a personal touch to their surroundings. Once making a quilt, hooking a rug, putting preserves by, were necessities. Then for a time such activities seemed quaint. Today personal creativity is to many a psychological necessity, and there is a special appeal in reinterpreting an old art/craft in a new way, as you will be able to do with the help of this book.

B.B.

Split Bars. Lancaster County,
Pennsylvania, circa 1890.
(Courtesy of America Hurrah Antiques)

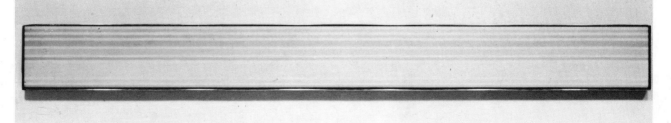

Kenneth Noland. *Via Pulse,* 1968. (Courtesy of André Emmerich Gallery)

The Amish and Their Quilts
by Jonathan Holstein

An immaculate Lancaster County, Pennsylvania, barn with a traditional Amish cart.

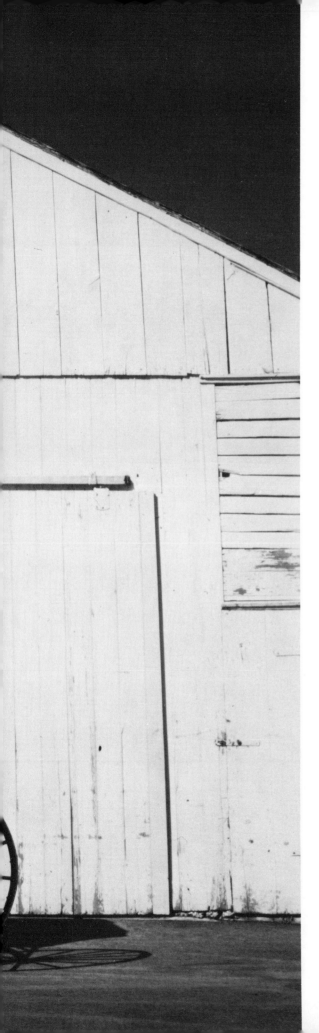

The Pennsylvania Amish, by keeping staunchly to their traditional ways, have unwittingly created a tourist industry. Busloads of people travel the narrow lanes of Lancaster County in all seasons to see the well-tended Amish farms, to catch a glimpse of the Amish riding in their buggies and working their fields with horse-drawn equipment, to see the Amish children on their way to one-room schools. These tableaux of rural life of an earlier era are outward signs of the survival of a radical religious tradition, one that has lasted over three centuries.

The Amish genesis was in the religious and social upheavals marking the breakup of the medieval world. In 1525, eight years after Luther posted his theses in Wittenberg, there arose the Swiss Brethren, later called Mennonites after Menno Simons, a Dutch reformer. The Brethren were part of the Anabaptist movement, the most radical edge of the emergent Protestant spectrum. Anabaptists rejected infant baptism and held that each person was directly accountable to his Maker. They wished a return to an earlier style of Christianity in which a brotherhood of mutually supportive believers would live in obedience to the Sermon on the Mount, rejecting worldly standards and values. They refused to take oaths or bear arms or respond violently to violence, and they put conscience before civil obedience.

These beliefs and practices, shared with some variations by a number of Anabaptist groups, put the Anabaptists at odds with the old Roman Catholic establishment, with the newer Protestant establishment, and with civil authority. Many, Martin Luther among them, thought the Anabaptists dangerous, and repression followed. Many groups disappeared or were scattered. Some Swiss Brethren fled the country; others settled in the mountains, and there the Amish sect eventually came into being.

In the last decade of the seventeenth century, one of the Swiss Brethren, Jacob Amman, became the leader of the conservative side in a doctrinal controversy. While several practices were in dispute, Amman made the strict observance of shunning—the avoidance by church members of an excommunicant—the major issue. Taking upon himself the mission of testing the rest of the leaders of the Brethren for orthodoxy and excommunicating on his own authority, he created a schism from which the Amish emerged. Amman left Switzerland for Alsace, beginning a series of Amish migrations that continued into the nineteenth century.

As early as 1683 there had been Mennonite emigration to the New World; a group settled in that year in Germantown, Pennsylvania. (This group had the distinction five years later of issuing the first protest against slavery in North America.) The first record of an American Amish settlement dates from about 1727. In Pennsylvania the Amish found two things of crucial importance to the survival and development of their culture: freedom from religious persecution and abundant rich land for farming. Here they could create Amish farming communities and follow in concert their religious and social customs.

The first Amish settlers came from Switzerland. Later Amish immigrants in the eighteenth and nineteenth centuries had roots in a number of other European countries—France, Alsace, Russia, and the Netherlands. They settled not only in Pennsylvania but also in Ohio, Illinois, Nebraska, Iowa, Kansas, South Dakota, and in

Ontario, Canada. Their pattern of life as it had developed in the Old World—self-reliant families for whom hard work and thrift were basic tenets and agriculture the main occupation—was to prove highly successful in the New World. As the Amish prospered in America, their remaining communities in Europe were disappearing, and now the Amish are to be found only on this continent.

Nonconformity is central to Amish life: living in the world but avoiding its sinful ways. This has from the beginning set them apart from many of their neighbors in America. Their continued use of German, their avoidance of modern conveniences such as electrical and engine power and machinery, their distinctive clothing, hair, and beard styles (little changed in a century), their banning of buttons—these are the outward manifestations of their apartness, and they serve to help maintain within the group its common identity and sense of purpose.

There is no central authority determining overall Amish social and religious practice. Instead, the society is broken into units somewhat determined by geography (for example, the practical length of carriage rides between members' houses, where services are held). Each group vests authority in a bishop chosen by its members from among its members and establishes its own *ordnungs*, or rules of social practice. These can reach as far into daily life as, for instance, to determine "proper" clothing colors. All groups, however, are in principle and fundamental practice united. And the outer surface of their lives is basically the same, best described as "plain": no personal adornment, clothing of a common style and of sensible and practical materials and cut. In their homes cleanliness and orderliness are the chief decorations, although an occasional fancy towel, a calendar with a picture, or a cupboard of fancy china can be seen.

This is a sharp contrast to neighbors of the Amish, the "gay" Dutch of Pennsylvania. (Pennsylvania "Dutch," a corruption of *Deutsch*, is a catchall term for many different groups that settled in Pennsylvania, their main link being the German language.) At one end of the scale are the Amish and the plainer of the Mennonite sects, who are close to the Amish in philosophy and practice. At the other end are those Dutch whose exuberant approach to life has produced Pennsylvania folk art, with its abundance of gay and amusing motifs and joyous colors. The homes and furnishings of the gay Dutch abound with such designs.

Naturally, there has been some interchange over the years between the plain and gay folk. While agriculture has remained their principal occupation—and the one most suited to maintaining their way of life—economic necessity has forced some Amish to take jobs away from the farms. Complete self-sufficiency is impossible, and there has been continual contact for long periods between the Amish and their non-Amish neighbors, and with the outer world in general.

I t seems likely, for example, that quilt making was not a native Amish craft, but one they adopted from other groups after their arrival in America. Quilt making was not practiced in their areas of origin, and very few Amish quilts have appeared that date before the 1870s, a peak period for the production of American quilts. When they do appear, however, their style is unmistakably Amish.

My wife and I saw our first Amish quilt in 1968, spread over a bed in a small antique store. We had never seen another quilt like it: bold alternating red and green bars in the center bordered with a strong purple, the whole surrounded with a wide rust-red border and edged in green. It was smashing—serene and yet of great inten-

A Lancaster County sheep.

Opposite top right: Log Cabin-Straight Furrow. Pennsylvania, circa 1875. Cushion covers. (Courtesy of America Hurrah Antiques)

Above: Roman Stripe Variation. Ohio, circa 1910. (Courtesy of America Hurrah Antiques)

Above right: Early Federal quilt. Non-Amish, circa 1810−1820. Displays use of the center medallion plan, popular trailing vine, and appliquéd sawtooth borders, printed cottons. (Courtesy of Metropolitan Museum of Art)

Right: Courthouse Steps Variation. Indiana, circa 1885. (Courtesy of America Hurrah Antiques)

sity and passion. We bought it and took it home, thinking at first it was just a single quilt maker's invention.

As we searched further in Amish areas, we began to see more of their quilts, and we realized that our first quilt was one of a large body of such work. We found that the Pennsylvania Amish made quilts in a limited range of patterns. Some of them, such as Sawtooth, Crazy, and Nine-Patch Block, they shared with their non-Amish neighbors. A few, such as the central Diamond and Bars, were unique to them. These designs were used over and over so they seem to be a series of proportion and color variations on set formats, much like Josef Albers's variations on the square. While the Amish shared with other Pennsylvania quilt makers the ability to make unlikely and startling color combinations work aesthetically, their results were more subtle and refined.

Generally the Amish preferred designs with large elements and they pieced them on machines. Part of the reason for this was, no doubt, their keen sense of time and work values. Large pieces can be quickly made into a top, and a foot-operated sewing machine will do the job in a fraction of the time hand-piecing takes. There is also the matter of worldliness. Piecing intricate and involved patterns might have smacked too much of worldly pride. (Indeed, in several areas of the Midwest, Amish leaders forbade piecing.) I believe it is for the same reason that almost no Amish quilts are appliquéd. The rarely seen Amish appliqué work is usually an addition to a pieced quilt. Cloth stitched onto other cloth just for decoration would seem wasteful and worldly.

Quilting, however, was a different matter. Amish quilting is at its worst good, and at its best superb. The stitching is fine, the motifs carefully planned and often elaborate. There are flowing feathers in borders; little "hex signs," pinwheels, hearts, and stars in corners; large stars often surrounded by feather wreaths in centers. In the later quilts appear stalks of roses, or roses and tulips growing from the same stalk or vine—an intricate assemblage of decorative and symbolic motifs used also by other Pennsylvania Dutch quilters, but never with the same overall harmony. I think it likely that such fancy work was allowed because it is not so visible, the quilting forming a subdued secondary pattern on the surface. Also, quilting was usually a shared task among the Amish, a quiet time during which relatives and friends could talk while, in the Amish way, keeping their hands always busy. Such pleasant tasks are often prolonged.

The majority of Pennsylvania quilts (indeed, of all surviving American quilts) are made of cotton and are stuffed with cotton. In an earlier America, however, before the advent of cheap cottons and cotton batting, wool quilts stuffed with wool were common. The Amish retained this tradition well into the twentieth century, using for the tops of their quilts very fine wools, and for the batting, wools of various fineness.

Colors are for the most part intense and somber—reds, greens, blues, shades of violet—generally, the earlier the quilt, the more somber the colors. The wools are unpatterned because the Amish considered patterned material worldly and used little of it. These wools take the light differently than cottons. They can absorb vast amounts of light without washing out visually. Instead, they become more intense and, in dim light, they seem to have an inner

14

The Amish still travel around the countryside in horse-drawn buggies.

Left: Thousands of Pyramids. Indiana, circa 1900. (Courtesy of America Hurrah Antiques)

Below: Double Irish Chain Variation. Ohio, circa 1910. (Courtesy of America Hurrah Antiques)

Bottom left: Chained Nine-Patch. Pennsylvania, circa 1895. (Courtesy of America Hurrah Antiques)

Bottom right: Log Cabin-Barn Raising. Pennsylvania, circa 1880. (Courtesy of George E. Schoellkopf Gallery)

Early autumn on an Amish farm.

Geese in a barnyard.

glow. The effect, in conjunction with the large geometric forms, is one of great elegance and strength.

Occasionally colors that seem quite gay are used—pinks, magentas, light blues, and greens—but such hues also appear in Amish clothing. In 1872 Phebe Gibbons described some Amish women she saw at a train station. One was wearing a ". . . gray shawl, brown stuff dress, purple apron. One young girl wore a bright-brown sunbonnet, a green dress, and a light blue apron." And at an Amish meeting: "The women, whom I have sometimes seen with a bright purple apron, an orange neckerchief, or some other striking bit of color, were now more soberly arrayed in plain white caps without ruffle or border, and white neckerchiefs, though occasionally a cap or kerchief was black."

It is my feeling that these were common materials and clothing colors of the period, and the Amish simply went on using them after others had followed changing fashion. Now Amish women use synthetic materials, often in colors similar to their traditional wools. Synthetics first appeared in Pennsylvania Amish quilts in the 1920s, often in conjunction with wools, to which they offer startling visual contrasts.

Midwestern Amish quilts are in all ways—materials, colors, patterns, and quilting—different from Amish quilts of Pennsylvania. Yet they, too, are unmistakably Amish. The quilting tradition began even later in the Midwest, and Amish quilts from that area seem to have been made largely of cotton. Starting in the twentieth century, the Midwest Amish especially liked a kind of cotton sateen, often used in black as a background color with a pieced block-style design in only one other color, a deep red or blue or green. The Midwest Amish were unique in their use of black as a basic quilt color and were particularly skilled at handling that and other dark tonalities, sometimes in contrast with each other, sometimes in combination with light and bright colors that were not used in Pennsylvania quilts. The sateens have some of the light-handling quality of the wools favored in Pennsylvania; that is, they are not highly reflective.

The Midwest Amish designs are not as unusual as are some of those of Pennsylvania but are an assortment of common designs used by many American quilt makers. The quilting patterns, too, are similar to those of their non-Amish neighbors, but, as in Pennsylvania Amish quilting, the technique is usually fine. While the basic design elements in Midwest Amish quilts are different from those of Pennsylvania, the effect is broadly the same. One is struck by their richness, elegance, and harmony. Together, Amish quilts from the two areas are the most intense of all American work and contain the most interesting color inventions.

The Amish had produced a good number of quilts over the years. In addition to the quilts they made for their own use, Amish women often furnished each of their children (and families were—and are—large) with one or more quilts to take with them when they left to start homes of their own. The number of older quilts in the Amish communities has, however, been much reduced. Normal wear and tear took their toll (the wool quilts of Pennsylvania were particularly susceptible to moth damage and more difficult to wash successfully than cotton quilts). And in recent years these earlier quilts have been heavily collected; a large percentage of what remained has passed into public and private collections.

Of course, the Amish did not simply stop making quilts. Quilt making has remained a popular craft among them. And, responding to the greatly increased interest in and demand for quilts, some Amish women have been making them for sale. Few, however, are made in the traditional, unique designs, or with the old-style materials.

A country stream running clear and undisturbed.

A restored late eighteenth-century Pennsylvania stone farmhouse.

Airing a quilt prolongs its life.

A covered bridge in Pennsylvania.

Jonathan Holstein and his wife, Gail van der Hoof, were pioneers in the appreciation of American quilts as serious design. He has lectured and written on the subject; his book, The Pieced Quilt *(New York Graphic Society), is a study of the origins and design basis of quilts in America. The Holsteins' quilt collection is one of the most important in the country.*

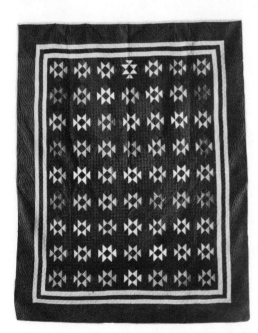

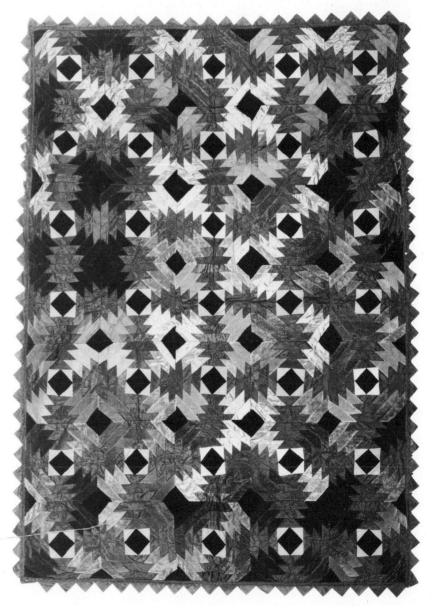

Top left: Diamond in the Square Variation. Lebanon County, Pennsylvania, circa 1880. (Courtesy of America Hurrah Antiques)

Top right: Bear's Paw. Ohio, circa 1915. (Courtesy of America Hurrah Antiques)

Above: Hovering Hawk Variation. Ohio, circa 1910. (Courtesy of America Hurrah Antiques)

Right: Log Cabin-Windmill. Ohio, circa 1890. (Courtesy of America Hurrah Antiques)

An Amish family out for a stroll.

Basics for Needlepointing Amish Quilts

Even if this is your first attempt at needlepoint, there is no reason why you cannot make a beautiful piece you will always enjoy having. Of course, the more needlepoint you do, the better your work will become. Your stitching motions, awkward at first, will become automatic. You will become adventurous about trying new stitches, and you will probably become so confident that you will want to improvise your own designs.

If you should have any difficulty in mastering a new stitch in this book, practice it on a separate piece of canvas until you are totally satisfied. Even if you are an accomplished needleworker, you will probably learn some new stitches from this book or certainly new ways of combining them in patterns.

If the work ever becomes tedious or frustrating, put it down and return to it later when you are relaxed again. Needlework should always be a pleasure, and compulsive people should try hard to curb their impatience to finish quickly.

No matter how little or how much needlepoint you have done, always take the time to observe good working habits:

Buy the best materials you can—canvas, yarn, needle—to complement the precious time and energy you will invest in your work.

Remove a misplaced stitch or poorly worked area as soon as you discover it. If you allow it to remain, every time you look at the work you will focus on that error. There are times, however, when you may make a small, almost imperceptible error and not realize it until you have completed the entire canvas. If the effect is minimal, it is usually not worth correcting.

You can work needlepoint on a frame, on rollers, or just in your hands. Never use a hoop unless it is large enough to hold the entire working surface well inside plus blank canvas surrounding the stitched area. Otherwise the pressure of the hoop could ruin your worked stitches.

Supplies

No matter which designs you work in this book, you will need the same basic supplies: canvas, yarn or thread, needles, scissors, seam ripper and tweezers (for removing incorrect stitching), masking tape.

Canvas

In the needlepoint vocabulary the word *mesh* is a synonym for the word *thread*. Canvas for needlepoint is made up of mesh or threads running horizontally and vertically. It is classified by the number of mesh or threads per inch, or the number of spaces or holes per inch.

A canvas having twenty-four mesh to an inch—#24 canvas—would be suitable for delicate and detailed petit point, while a canvas with only three or four mesh to an inch—#3 canvas or #4 canvas—is fine for a heavy latch-hooked rug. In our designs we most often used #12, #13, and #14 canvases. There are many people who prefer to work on #10 canvas. This canvas can be used for all of our Amish designs. The finished size will be larger, so you will need a larger piece of canvas, and the stitches will require more yarn. In our project section we used other canvas sizes: #24 (left top) for a petit point dollhouse rug or wall hanging; #16 (left center) for pillows out of velvet yarn; #7 for large wall hangings; #6 for a rug; and #3½ rug canvas (left bottom) for a latch-hooked rug.

The mesh of the canvas can be either mono (single thread) or Penelope (double threads). Penelope is most useful for combining petit point with continental, half-cross, or basketweave. All our canvas needlework was done on mono interlocked. Mono threads can separate or pull apart easily; the mono interlocked threads do not. In mono interlocked the warp threads, which run vertically and parallel to the selvage, are twisted; the weft threads run horizontally through the twists of the warp. Unless a loop where the weft runs through the twist in the warp is cut, you cannot pull the threads apart. The interlocked canvas is therefore very sturdy. Most work on interlocked canvas does not require extensive blocking.

Note of caution: In researching this book we discovered that many manufacturers, unfortunately, sell needlepoint canvas in sizes that are approximate rather than exact. We worked needlepoints on canvas that we thought had fourteen spaces to the inch, then measured and found only thirteen. In the past year a new label has become available that reads True #14. Buy this type of #14 canvas if it is available in your needlework shop, and always measure any canvas before you purchase it.

You can buy canvas ranging in width from approximately 27 inches to 40 inches. Wider canvas can be ordered specially. Most stores will sell canvas by the yard, and many sell as little as one quarter of a yard. If you do not need the entire width for a single project, save your scraps. They are useful for small projects such as coasters, pincushions, and eyeglass cases, and they are also good for practicing stitches.

Always check canvas before you buy it to be sure it has no knots or flaws that could later split and destroy your finished work.

Yarn

The most versatile wool yarn and the one that comes in a selection of the most vibrant dyes is the Persian. This is the yarn we used most frequently in our Amish designs. (Only the special projects use other yarns and threads.) Each full Persian strand is made up of three threads, which separate easily. The full three-ply strand will normally cover a #12 mono canvas (opposite left top), but this will depend partly on your individual stitching tension. If you pull the yarn tightly, you may have to add an extra strand that you have separated from the twist of three to cover the mesh completely. If you work too loosely, the yarn will sag and not form a neat design. Try to develop a consistent stitching technique in the correct tension.

The canvas size you select, the types of stitches you plan to work, and the finished size of your needlework will determine the amount of yarn or thread you need to buy. It is a good idea to stick to one brand of yarn for uniform weight and color. Always buy more yarn than you think you need because dye lots change, and it may be difficult to match the yarns later. (If you make a mistake and must

Approximately one-third actual size:

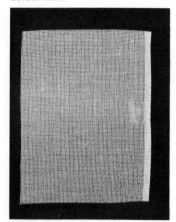

#24 mono canvas

#16 mono canvas

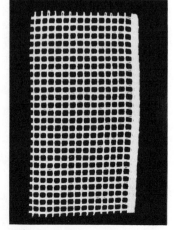

#3½ rug canvas

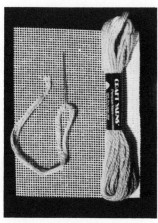

#12 mono interlocked canvas
with Craft Persian yarn

rip out yarn, do not reuse that yarn. Use new yarn.) Many companies now package Persian in a variety of quantities such as 6-, 10-, and 40-yard skeins. Most needlepoint shops sell yarn by the yard or by the ounce in a skein. Some even sell a few strands, which is helpful if you need to fill only a small area.

To calculate the amount of yarn needed, multiply the length and width of the area on your canvas you want to cover. Work a sample square inch and keep track of the amount of yarn used. Then multiply the square inches to be covered by the number of inches of wool your sample required. In each set of instructions for our Amish designs, we have listed how much yarn or thread we used. For the designs worked in Persian yarn, we chose the convenient measurement of 32-inch strands. The amounts needed for the special projects were listed according to the particular product used, sometimes again 32-inch strands, sometimes skeins, yards, or precut wool packs. Take a copy of our list when you purchase materials. The yarn salesperson will be able to translate requirements into the correct amounts according to the shop's way of selling.

Needles

Needlepoint needles, also called tapestry needles, have large eyes and blunt tips. They are available in any size for whatever yarn or thread and canvas size you are using. The eye of the needle must be large enough for the yarn to slip through. The needle should neither drop through the canvas hole nor have to be pulled or tugged. It should ride through easily. Generally, you will use a #18 or #20 needle for a #12 or #13 canvas, and a #20 needle for a #14 canvas. This is not a hard and fast rule because different manufacturers produce needles with slight variations. For example, some #18 needles are tapered enough to use on a #14 canvas.

There are two ways to thread a needle. The conventional way takes a little practice. Fold the yarn over the needle, held between thumb and index finger so that the yarn does not show on top. Grasp the needle with the other hand and pull it free. Place the eye of the needle over your fingers where the yarn is hidden and push the eye end down, separating the thumb and the index finger slightly until the yarn emerges threaded in the needle. Or you can make a needle threader. Using a color page from a magazine (it is usually heavier in weight than a black and white page) or a piece of loose-leaf paper, cut a piece approximately $3/4$ inch long and $1/2$ inch wide. Fold it lengthwise so that it now measures $3/4$ inch long and $1/4$ inch wide. Place the yarn in the fold, like a hot dog in a bun, keeping the tip of the yarn inside the paper. Push the yarn sandwich through the eye of the needle.

You can save time when working by keeping several needles threaded in a pincushion. For those patterns requiring numerous colors, make a color card. Take a sheet of paper and note the manufacturer's number for the color and the name of the color. Next to these tape a small piece of the yarn, and next to the yarn keep a threaded needle so that you need not constantly rethread.

Other equipment

Other useful equipment for needlepoint includes a small pair of sharp scissors for cutting yarn and a heavier pair for cutting canvas. Always have on hand a seam ripper and tweezers for ripping. Do not use scissors for ripping because you may cut into the mesh. If you accidentally cut the canvas you can mend it by making a patch on the back. (Using a small piece of excess canvas, match the warp and weft, baste around, weaving in and out, and then work your

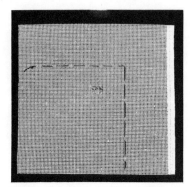

Basting stitches used to outline an area

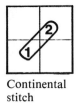

Continental stitch

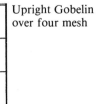

Upright Gobelin over four mesh

3	8	16	24	32	33	25	17	9	2	
11									6	
19									14	
27									22	
35									30	
34									31	
26									23	
18									15	
10									7	
1	5	13	21	29	36	28	20	12	4	

Rosebud over nine mesh

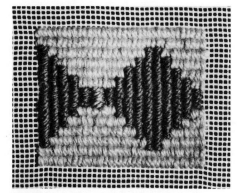

Gobelin stitch over two mesh worked both horizontally and vertically for Courthouse Steps needlepoint

design stitches through both pieces of canvas. Trim patch. Proceed to finish rest of design.)

Also have on hand 1-inch-wide masking tape for sealing raw mono canvas edges so they do not ravel. Sealing edges also prevents yarn from catching and fraying as you work.

Although you need not mark the canvases for our designs, you may feel more secure if you do so. The use of marking pens for outlining or coloring areas can present a problem, regardless of what the pen manufacturers claim. So-called permanent markers may come off on the yarn. Thoroughly test markers by using them on a piece of extra canvas and wetting the canvas. Sometimes it is not the marker that causes the problem. Canvases have different finishes or sizings. (These add strength to the canvas and make it smooth so that the needle can slide through the holes easily.) Some sizings cause the canvas to absorb the marker color and end up coloring the yarns. Other canvases repel the marker altogether. Basting stitches on the canvas serve the same purpose as outlining an area with a marker (left top). You can remove the basting stitches easily as you are finishing an area. If you must color areas, be sure to test both the canvas and the markers in advance.

Learning to stitch

Stitches can run in different directions on the canvas: horizontally, vertically, and diagonally. We have illustrated three stitches (left center) to help you learn to work different directions: a continental, an upright Gobelin over four mesh, and a rosebud over nine mesh. Each line on the graph equals one mesh on the canvas. The continental covers one mesh of the canvas on the diagonal; the Gobelin covers four vertical mesh; the rosebud covers a nine-mesh square.

Many stitches can be worked in two directions. For example, the Gobelin is used in the center design of the Courthouse Steps needlepoint *both* horizontally and vertically (left below).

The numbers on the stitches here and in our complete instructions and stitch glossary tell you how to work it. The *odd number* represents the space (hole between the mesh) from which the needle and yarn emerge from the back up through the front of the canvas. The *even number* represents the hole through which you return the needle to the back of the canvas after covering some of the threads. Working one continental or one Gobelin stitch requires one up and one down motion. Completing one rosebud requires a series of motions, up on the odd numbers, down on the even numbers.

Using the stitch glossary on pages 28–31, which illustrates the basic stitches of needlepoint, practice some more stitches on a canvas scrap if they are new to you: the continental both horizontally and vertically, the upright Gobelin over three and four mesh, the upright Gobelin in a diagonal progression, and another rosebud. You will soon get the feeling of working the stitches. Always practice on the same size mesh and with the same yarn and needle you plan to use for your Amish project. If you want more practice after you feel comfortable working several different stitches, choose a graph in the instruction section and work a portion of it. In this way you will become familiar with working different stitches on one canvas.

When two areas with stitches in different directions converge, coverage can be a problem. You will sometimes have to compensate by covering the mesh with small stitches. For example, in Nine-Patch (pages 76–79) you must work a row of continental stitches along the sides between areas (4) and (5).

Always follow the numbers on the stitch diagrams. They give the order of working that stitch. There are two schools of thought on working a stitch: in one movement (in and out) or in two movements (inserting the needle from front to back, then from back to front). The consensus is that you should do whichever feels most comfortable. Those needleworkers opposed to the first method claim that the yarn gets too much wear and frays too quickly. Yet the basketweave, one of the sturdiest stitches, is usually worked in this manner.

Beginning to stitch

Now you are ready to undertake an Amish quilt in needlepoint. Cut your canvas according to our directions. Using dark sewing thread or extra yarn, mark off 3 inches of blank canvas all around the edges with basting stitches. If you want your finished piece to be 14 inches by 14 inches, your canvas should measure 20 inches by 20 inches. The usual allowance of 1 to 2 inches at the edge is too meager if blocking is necessary. Do not permit a framer or upholsterer to cut off the extra canvas when it is prepared for use in your home.

Tape the raw edges of your canvas so that the threads do not unravel (on mono canvas) and so that the yarn does not catch on the edges and fray as you work the canvas. For this purpose use 1-inch-wide masking tape, folding it over both the front and the back of the canvas. Be sure to put the selvage on the right or the left side and mark "Top" in pencil on the masking tape.

Make a color guide, noting the names of the colors and the manufacturer's numbers in case you need more yarn or want to use that color again in the future.

Cut yarn or threads into 18-inch lengths. Longer strands will fray and become thin as you stitch, and then they will not cover the canvas mesh completely.

When starting work on a blank canvas, leave a short tail of yarn (1 or 2 inches) as you pull the needle and yarn up to the front. You will work your next few stitches over that tail in the back. When starting a new thread on a canvas that already has some worked areas, work the tail through some of the threads on the back. When you are finished with an area, run your yarn through several stitches (about ½ inch) on the back of the canvas to secure it and cut it off close to the canvas so it will not be caught as you continue to work. Try to make the back as neat as the front. If you are working the basketweave stitch, lightly catch the yarn on the back of the canvas, or else you will make ridges on the front that cannot be corrected when the canvas is blocked.

Use the complete strand of Persian or Persian-type yarn, but we recommend that first you take the three-part strand, separate it, and then gather it back together. You will achieve better coverage this way. When working the continental or basketweave, use only two parts of the original strand. Other exceptions will be noted in our instructions. Caution: Colors dye differently, and yarns of different colors therefore have different weights. If a yarn is too thin, add another ply so that you can cover the canvas completely. If the yarn is too thick, subtract one of the plies.

When working, allow the threaded needle to dangle frequently. This unwinds the yarn and prevents if from becoming too thin.

When not working the canvas, secure the needle outside the working area. Changes in the weather could cause the mesh to hold the raised shape where the needle was.

Outline of the Streak of Lightning needlepoint

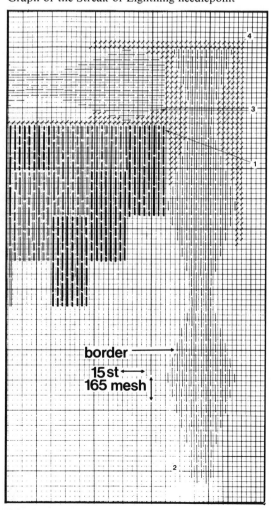

Graph of the Streak of Lightning needlepoint

border
15 st
165 mesh

Store your yarn neatly. Make a slip knot of the yarn through a hoop. Taking a strand off is easy, and this hoop is portable.

Using our instructions

The instructions for our needlepoints give every step in sequence so that a beginner as well as an advanced needleworker can attempt any of the patterns with success. Whichever design you choose to execute, follow the rules for *that* design. Each example includes an *outline* (left top) that gives the stitch (keyed by letter), the colors (by uncircled number), and the consecutive order of working the design (circled numbers). There is also a *graph* (left below) that gives the stitches (their placement on the canvas, how many mesh they cover, in which direction they run, where to start each major area). Each set of instructions also includes a list of the *stitches* necessary to complete the needlepoint, a set of detailed suggestions on the *method of working* the needlepoint, and a *color list* (with the names of colors, manufacturer's numbers, and amounts needed).

The photograph of the almost finished Streak of Lightning needlepoint illustrates many of these steps (opposite top). Begin working in area (1) near the upper right-hand corner of the center area. For the entire center area use one stitch—the diamond satin in a 2-4-6-4-2 vertical pattern—in a series of black and red streaks. After you finish this area, work one row of continental stitches across the top and across the bottom of area (1). Next proceed to area (2), where you use the Parisian stitch in an elongated diamond shape. Begin the Parisian stitch in the middle of the right-hand side. After you complete Parisian stitches on all four sides, surround them with continental stitches, in area (3).

Finally work area (4), which is the border, two rows of continental or basketweave stitches on every side. If you are using the basketweave, work the area across the top first from right to left, then down the sides from top to bottom, and finally across the bottom from right to left. To work the continental stitch around, start at the right side and work the vertical continental down with the first row touching the finished needlepoint. Turn the needlepoint upside down and work the second row of vertical continental down. Next work the left side in the same manner. Now move to the bottom of the needlepoint and use the horizontal continental across, from right to left. Work the second row after you have turned the canvas. Proceed to the top of the needlepoint. Turn the needlepoint upside down, and work the two rows of horizontal continental across. Turning the needlepoint enables you to work from an empty space to an occupied space, which is easier. Slant all of your continental stitches in the same direction unless instructions state otherwise.

In every Amish design except Railroad Crossing, you will begin by working toward the center area of the canvas or by working in the center area. Later you will work the remaining areas. We have found that this procedure eliminates many errors.

Several of the needleworkers who made our Amish design samples departed from the directions to some degree without catastrophic results. Case in point: the finished Nine-Patch needlepoint differs from the graph in the number of ovals surrounding the central area, yet the finished product is just as lovely. The object is to enjoy the projects whether you follow our instructions to a tee or improvise your own designs, as this sample maker did.

Special projects

The project section includes complete instructions for working two new designs—Four-Patch in velvet yarn (Veloura) and a Sunshine

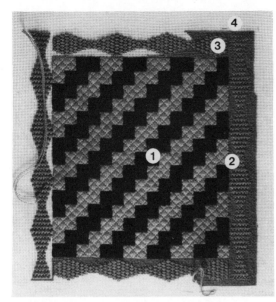

Circled numbers on the Streak of Lightning needlepoint indicate order in which to work areas of canvas

---

Essentials for working an Amish design:

1. In each set of instructions, look for an *outline* that gives the stitch (keyed by letter), the colors (by uncircled number), the consecutive order of working the design (circled numbers). There is a *graph* that diagrams the stitches (placement on canvas, how many mesh covered, stitch direction, where to start each major area). Also included: a set of detailed suggestions on the *method of working;* a *color list; stitch diagrams.*

2. Tape raw edges of canvas with 1-inch-wide masking tape. With pencil mark "Top" of canvas on tape.

3. Measure the design onto canvas, marking perimeter with sewing thread. Always leave 3 inches of blank canvas as a border.

4. Before threading needle, separate each ply of the three-ply strand of yarn. Place strands parallel to each other, gather together, thread needle. Note how many plies each stitch calls for. When working the continental or basketweave, use only two plies of original strand. Other exceptions will be noted.

5. When working, allow threaded needle to dangle often to untwist.

6. Keep tension even when stitching.

7. When not working, secure the needle outside the working area of canvas.

8. Always roll canvas, never fold it.

9. Most designs do not need blocking, just light steaming. Place design on a Turkish towel, right side down. Hold steam iron at appropriate setting 2 inches above needlepoint. Let steam penetrate. Smooth canvas with hand.

---

and Shadow or Trip Around the World in embroidery thread. The other six projects are adaptations of the needlepoints seen elsewhere in the book: Split Bars worked in pearl cotton #1; Stars and Stripes in rug yarn; Railroad Crossing in velvet yarn; Rainbow in acrylic yarn; Baskets or Cake Stand in pearl cotton #3; Checkerboard as a latch-hooked rug.

Converting stitches to continental

You can work all of the needlepoints in this book exclusively in the basic continental stitch or basketweave if you desire. We have included instructions on page 83 to explain how.

Additional stitches

There are many stitches in the needlework repertoire that we did not use in our twenty-seven designs but that could be employed. We have included diagrams on pages 128–131 of a few of these for your future work.

Leaving your monogram

As you complete your needlepoint, you may want to add your initials and the date you finished the work. For that reason we have included alphabets in upper- and lowercase letters and numerals in stitch design. You can leave a small box in a corner or extend the border. You can also work the monogram on a backing made entirely of needlepoint stitches which is the same size as your Amish needlepoint design. Sew these two pieces together as a pillow or soft tapestry so that both sides can be visible. See pages 132–139.

Framing

Whatever project you work, you will not want any of the design eliminated when you turn the canvas into pillow, picture, or rug. It is for this reason that you add at least two rows of continental stitch or basketweave on every side. Special tips on framing:

Always measure your finished piece of needlework before framing. Give these measurements to your framer so that he knows the exact size you wish to retain. Otherwise he may overstretch your work and expose the canvas. Because of the stress, the yarn may pop.

Many needlepoint shops and framers know how to block your work correctly. Upholsterers and fine cleaners also do blocking. It can also be a do-it-yourself project. Many craft books offer excellent blocking directions, and we list a few in our bibliography.

To cover with glass or not? The pros and cons are about equal. The argument against is that since wool breathes and responds to changes in humidity, heat, and pollution and has texture and depth, it is an unsound practice to cover and flatten it. Glass opponents are also usually against spraying finished works with dirt-retardant solutions because the addition of chemicals to the yarns will eventually damage them. The pro-glass people claim that dirt will accumulate and become too embedded in the work to remove. The large needlepoint tapestries in churches, temples, and museums are vacuumed about every six months and when necessary are washed with a special solution. (And no one will divulge the secret formula.) If you must dry-clean your work, make sure that it will not be steam pressed. This flattens the stitches so much that your work will resemble cardboard. Whether or not you cover your needlepoint with glass should depend upon personal choice tempered by the consideration of where you will hang it (in a kitchen, cover it; in a living room it may not be necessary), the area where you live (in a city, yes; in the country, no), and the effect you want to achieve.

Stitch
Glossary

These are the basic stitches of needlepoint and are the stitches we used most in our Amish canvas work designs. They are all easy to master if you follow the numbers and remember that various stitches cover different numbers of canvas mesh. Each line on the graph equals one mesh or thread on a canvas. Always bring the threaded needle up through the canvas space at 1 (odd), insert the needle down through the space at 2 (even), up at 3 (odd), and so on. Every stitch will share a space with another stitch, producing a tightly woven surface. The number of mesh you cover and the direction in which you stitch will create different textures. Compensating stitches are necessary with some of the stitches to complete an area. When shown, they are indicated by the symbol θ and letters instead of numbers.

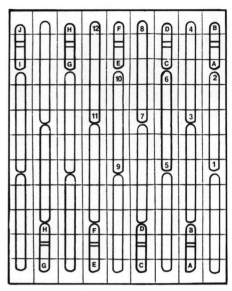

Large brick, pattern I

You can work this stitch vertically as here or horizontally as in large brick, pattern II. In this example each stitch covers four mesh, but they alternate in placement, making the pattern resemble a neatly laid brick wall. (Large brick stitches can cover up to six mesh.) Remember to work the pattern from right to left and then from left to right in alternate rows. The smaller stitches at the top and at the bottom are compensating stitches.

Small brick, pattern II

This stitch runs horizontally as does large brick, pattern II, but it covers two mesh instead of four mesh.

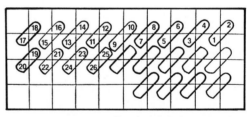

Continental, horizontal

The continental, one of the basic slanting stitches, is usually worked horizontally from right to left. The canvas can be turned upside down for alternate rows. It is best to use it only when you are filling in small areas because it distorts the canvas when worked over a large area.

Continental, vertical

The continental can also be worked in a vertical fashion. Stitch from top to bottom. You can turn canvas upside down for alternate rows. Use it as you would the horizontal continental, sparingly.

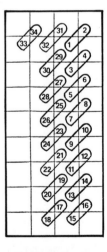

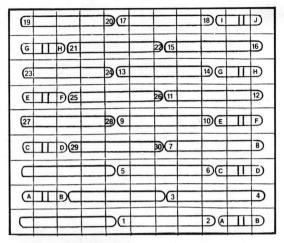

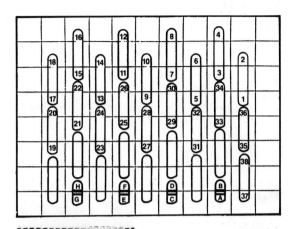

Large brick, pattern II

This stitch again covers four mesh and alternates in placement, but it differs from pattern I in that it runs horizontally instead of vertically. As you will see from the numbers, you work one series from bottom to top and then the next series from top to bottom.

Small brick, pattern I

Like large brick, pattern I, these stitches run vertically. Each covers two mesh.

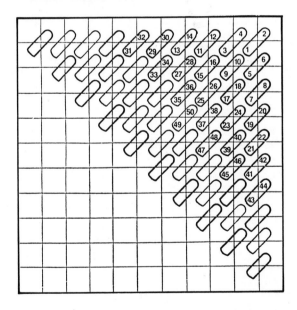

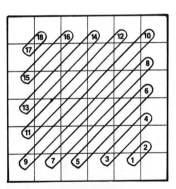

Basketweave

Also called diagonal continental, the basketweave is a sturdy stitch that produces the least pull on the canvas. It is therefore good for filling in large background areas. The name derives from the woven pattern it forms on the back of the canvas. Work it from the upper right-hand corner, following the numbers.

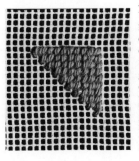

Scotch

The Scotch pattern is made of slanting stitches worked over varying numbers of mesh to produce a square. In this pattern begin in the lower right corner. First work over one mesh on the diagonal, then two, then three, then four, then five, and then back down to one mesh at top left.

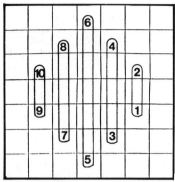

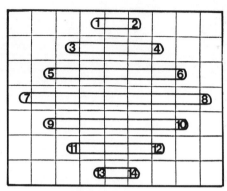

Diamond satin, 2-4-6-4-2
vertical pattern

Diamond satin, 2-4-6-8-6-4-2
vertical pattern

Diamond satin, 2-4-6-8-6-4-2
horizontal pattern

Diamond satin

In this variation of a Hungarian bargello stitch, the stitches alternate in height and direction, but they always form diamonds. When several diamonds are worked together, the pattern approximates waffle quilting. This stitch covers the canvas fairly quickly.

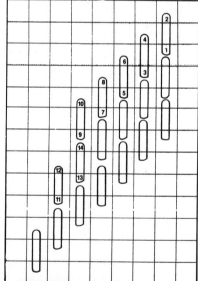

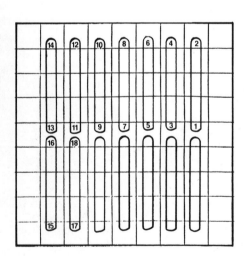

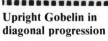

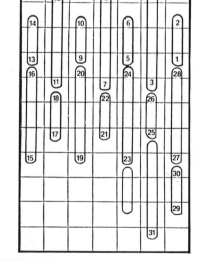

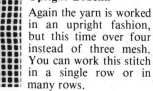

Upright Gobelin

Again the yarn is worked in an upright fashion, but this time over four instead of three mesh. You can work this stitch in a single row or in many rows.

Upright Gobelin in diagonal progression

The upright Gobelin can also be worked in an upward or downward progression to resemble a diagonal line.

Parisian

Like the upright Gobelin, this pattern consists of long stitches worked vertically. It can also be worked horizontally. Here, however, the stitches vary in length.

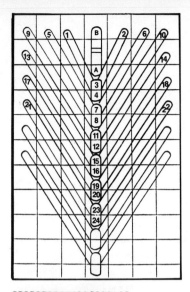

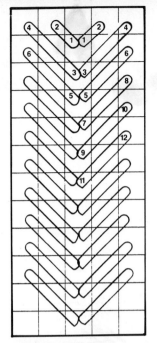

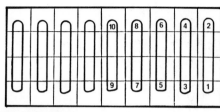

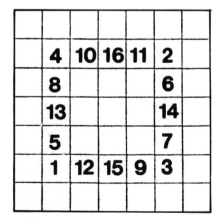

Fly

The fly stitch is used most often in embroidery work. It adds a handsome texture when used in needlepoint, especially for borders. You can work it over varying widths of mesh; here it covers six mesh across. Bring the needle up at 1; go down at 2 loosely, leaving a loop; come up at 3, catch the loop, and tighten the yarn; and go down at 4. Then begin again at 5 the same way. Use a compensating stitch at the top to even off the row. You can use the fly in a single stripe or side by side, depending upon the width you are covering.

Stem

The stem stitch, like the fly stitch, is best for a border. It consists of rows of slanting stitches. Work one side and then the other. Note that the first stitches in this pattern cover only one mesh while the successive stitches cover two mesh.

Upright Gobelin

The Gobelin is a good stitch for working yarn vertically (as here, over three mesh), horizontally, or diagonally. Be sure to follow the numbers when stitching. Always go from 2 to 3 rather than "cheating" and going from 2 to 4 and then down to 3. The yarn will lie more smoothly and will not twist.

4	10	16	11	2	
8				6	
13				14	
5				7	
1	12	15	9	3	

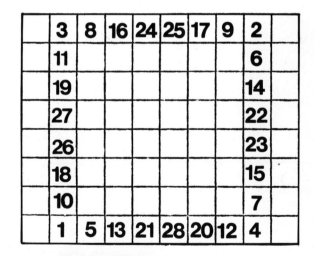

3	8	16	24	25	17	9	2	
11							6	
19							14	
27							22	
26							23	
18							15	
10							7	
1	5	13	21	28	20	12	4	

Double leviathan

This stitch produces a raised texture. Bring the yarn and needle up at 1 and down at 2, then up at 3 and down at 4, and so on. You are making a series of cross-stitches which, when worked over and over each other, produce a raised texture that is a nice contrast to rows of flat stitches.

Rosebud

The rosebud is another raised stitch in which you cross the yarn or threads. Follow the numbers. The size of the square can vary. Here it is over seven vertical and seven horizontal mesh.

When the patchwork was completed, it was laid flatly on the lining (often another expanse of patchwork), with layers of wool or cotton wadding between, and the edges were basted all around. Four bars of wood, about ten feet long, "the quiltin'-frame," were placed at the four edges, the quilt was sewed to them with stout thread, the bars crossed and tied firmly at corners, and the whole raised on chairs or tables to a convenient height. Thus around the outstretched quilt a dozen quilters could sit running the whole together with fanciful set designs of stitching. When about a foot on either side was wholly quilted, it was rolled upon its bar, and the work went on; thus the visible quilt diminished, like Balzac's Peau de Chagrin, in a united and truly sociable work that required no special attention, in which all were facing together and all drawing closer together as the afternoon passed in intimate gossip. Sometimes several quilts were set up. I know of a ten days' quilting bee in Narragansett in 1752.

From Alice Morse Earle, *Home Life in Colonial Days,* 1974.

The next sixteen pages illustrate the Amish-inspired needlepoints in color. For instructions on how to work the designs on canvas, see pages 50–127.

Opposite: Bars. Lancaster County, Pennsylvania, 1920–1925.
(Collection of Jonathan and Gail Holstein)

Above left: Sunshine and Shadow or Trip Around the World. Pennsylvania, circa 1930. (Sarah Melvin)
Above right: Rainbow. Pennsylvania but non-Amish, circa 1880. (Jonathan and Gail Holstein)
Below: Bars. Lancaster County, Pennsylvania, circa 1900. (Jonathan and Gail Holstein)

Opposite: Shadows. Indiana, circa 1890. (Phyllis Haders)

Right: Diamond. Lancaster County, Pennsylvania, circa 1930.
(Edward and Barbara Buchholz)
Below: Courthouse Steps. Pennsylvania, circa 1895. (America Hurrah Antiques)
Bottom: Bars. Pennsylvania, circa 1925. (Rhea Goodman)

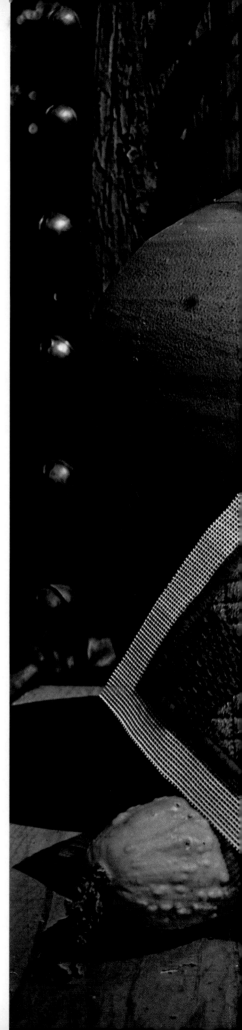

36

Above left: Split Bars. Lancaster County, Pennsylvania, circa 1900. (Jonathan and Gail Holstein)
Above right: Checkerboard. Ohio, circa 1890. (Jonathan and Gail Holstein)
Below: Single Irish Chain. Indiana, circa 1900. (Phyllis Haders)

Opposite: Nine-Patch. Lancaster County, Pennsylvania, circa 1910. (Phyllis Haders)

Above: Split Bars, special project #1 in pearl cotton #1, see page 82; in Persian yarn, see pages 80–82. Lancaster County, Pennsylvania, circa 1925. (Jonathan and Gail Holstein)

Below: Sunshine and Shadow or Trip Around the World, special project #2 in embroidery thread, see page 85. Pennsylvania, 1920–1925. (George E. Schoellkopf Gallery)

Right: Work these other special projects on different sizes of canvas and with different types of yarns. #3, Stars and Stripes in rug wool, page 86. #4, Railroad Crossing in velvet yarn, page 86. #5, Rainbow in acrylic rug yarn, pages 86–87. #6, Baskets or Cake Stand in pearl cotton #3, page 87. #7, Checkerboard in precut wool for a latch-hooked rug, see page 88. #8, Four-Patch in velvet yarn, pages 89–91. Lancaster County, Pennsylvania, 1880–1890. (America Hurrah Antiques)

40

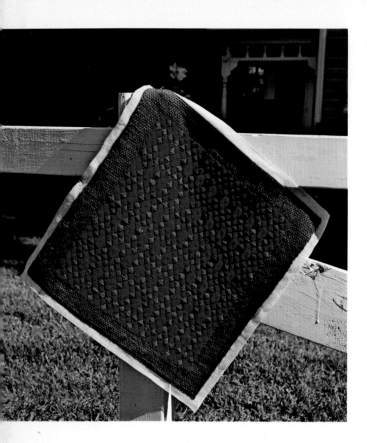

Above left: Improved Nine-Patch. Lancaster County, Pennsylvania, circa 1890. (Jonathan and Gail Holstein)
Above right: Variable Star. Ohio, circa 1900. (America Hurrah Antiques)
Below: Diamond. Lancaster County, Pennsylvania, circa 1910. (Jonathan and Gail Holstein)

Opposite: Lone Star. Indiana, circa 1930. (Arthur and Patricia Wilkins)

Left: Railroad Crossing. Holmes County, Ohio, circa 1930. (Jonathan and Gail Holstein)

Top: Log Cabin-Straight Furrow. Lancaster County, Pennsylvania, circa 1925. (Jonathan and Gail Holstein)

Above: Streak of Lightning. Pennsylvania, circa 1910. (Jonathan and Gail Holstein)

Above left: Stars and Stripes. Tuscarawas County, Ohio, circa 1920. (Phyllis Haders)
Above right: Baskets or Cake Stand. Lancaster County, Pennsylvania, circa 1920. (Jonathan and Gail Holstein)
Below: Baskets or Cake Stand. Pennsylvania, circa 1940. (Sarah Melvin)

Opposite: Baby's Block Variation. Illinois, circa 1910. (Jonathan and Gail Holstein)

A BLESSING OF WOMEN

By Stanley Kunitz

*"Remember me is all I ask,
And, if remembered be a task,
Forget me."*

—Album verses by Minerva Butler
Miller, tinsmith's daughter,
peddler's wife, c. 1850.

BLESS ZERUAH HIGLEY GUERNSEY
of Castleton, Vermont, who sheared the
wool from her father's sheep; washed,
carded, and spun it into yarn; steeped it in
dyes concocted from native berries, barks,
and plants; and embroidered it, in Double
Kensington chain stitch, on a ground of
homespun squares until they bloomed with
fruit, shells, snow crystals, flowers, and
cats, most singularly a noble blue cat; each
of the eighty-odd panels being different
from the rest, and the whole a paragon of
American needlework design, executed in
the ardor of her long pre-nuptial flight,
and accomplished in 1835 for her ill-starred
wedding day.

BLESS DEBORAH GOLDSMITH,
genteel itinerant, who supported her aged
and impoverished parents by traveling from
house to house in the environs of Hamilton,
New York, painting portraits of the
families who gave her bed and board, until
she limned in watercolors the likeness of
one George Throop, who married her,
therewith terminating her travels and
leading to her premature decease, at
twenty-seven.

BLESS MRS. AUSTIN ERNEST
of Paris, Illinois, whose husband, a local
politician of no other fame, organized in
1853 a rally for the Presidential candidate
of the new Republican party, following
which she gathered the material used to
decorate the stand wherefrom the immortal
Lincoln spoke and, with scissors and needle
and reverential heart, transformed it into a
quilted patchwork treasure.

BLESS MARY ANN WILSON,
who in 1810 appeared in the frontier town
of Greenville, New York, with her
"romantic attachment," a Miss Brundage,
with whom she settled in a log cabin,
sharing their lives and their gifts, Miss
Brundage farming the land, Miss Wilson
painting dramatic scenes with a bold hand,
in colors derived from berries, brickdust,
and store paint, and offering her

compositions for sale as "rare and unique
works of art."

BLESS HANNAH COHOON,
who dwelt in the Shaker "City of Peace,"
Hancock, Massachusetts, where a spirit
visited her, as frequently happened there,
and gave her "a draft of a beautiful Tree
pencil'd on a large sheet of white paper,"
which she copied out, not knowing till
later, with assistance from the Beyond, that
it was the Tree of Life; and who saw in
another vision, which she likewise
reproduced, the Elders of the community
feasting on cakes at a table beneath
mulberry trees; and who believed,
according to the faith of the followers of
Mother Ann Lee, that Christ would return
to earth in female form.

BLESS IN A CONGREGATION,
because they are so numerous, those
industrious schoolgirls stitching their
alphabets; and the deft ones with needles
at lacework, crewel, knitting; and mistresses
of spinning, weaving, dyeing; and
daughters of tinsmiths painting their
ornamental mottoes; and hoarders of rags
hooking and braiding their rugs; and adepts
in cutouts, valentines, stencils, still lifes,
and "fancy pieces"; and middle-aged
housewives painting, for the joy of it,
landscapes and portraits; and makers of
bedcovers with names that sing in the
night—Rose of Sharon, Princess Feather,
Delectable Mountains, Turkey Tracks,
Drunkard's Path, Indiana Puzzle, Broken
Dishes, Star of LeMoyne, Currants and
Coxcomb, Rocky-Road-to-Kansas.

BLESS THEM AND GREET THEM
as they pass from their long obscurity,
through the gate that separates us from our
history, a moving rainbow-cloud of
witnesses in a rising hubbub, jubilantly
turning to greet one another, this tumult
of sisters.

This prose was inspired by a show of
American folk art at the Whitney Museum
of American Art.

Opposite: Jake Mast.
Haven, Kansas,
circa 1935.
(Phyllis Haders)

Bars

In color, see page 33.

The bars at center are the focal point: alternating rows of turquoise diamond satin and purple continental.

Work the needlepoint on a piece of 19¼″ x 21″ #12 mono interlocked canvas. Approximate size of finished needlepoint is 13¼″ x 15″.

Circled numbers indicate order in which to work areas of canvas.
Letters indicate stitches with which to work areas of canvas.
Uncircled numbers indicate colors with which to work areas of canvas.

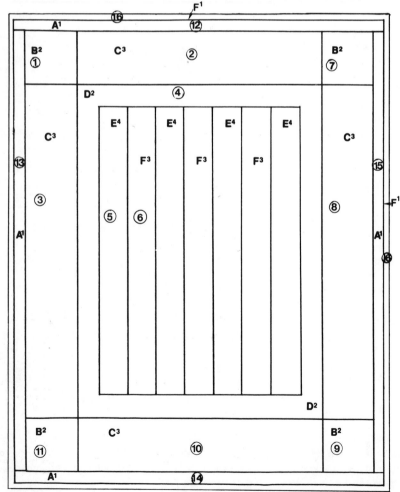

Outline

Stitches

A. fly, pattern II
B. large brick, pattern II
C. large brick, pattern I
D. small brick, pattern II
E. diamond satin, 2-4-6-8-6-4-2 vertical pattern
F. continental or basketweave

Suggested method of working this pattern

For all stitches use the complete three-ply strand, except for the continental or basketweave which requires two plies. Area (1) is begun in upper left-hand corner. Use the large brick, pattern II. Turn the canvas one quarter clockwise to work this area easily. Work area (2) for 4 inches across the top using large brick, pattern I. Area (3) is large brick, pattern I, worked 4 inches down left side. Area (4) is small brick, pattern II. Start in upper left corner where areas (1), (2), and (3) meet. Work across 4 inches, as far as you have worked area (2). Note: Be sure to work beginning stitches as on graph (opposite top). Stitches share same space. Work area (4) down left side for 4 inches. Areas (5) and (6) form the center design area and consist of seven bars. Alternate one bar of diamond satin, 2-4-6-8-6-4-2 vertical pattern (opposite below), with a bar of continental or basketweave stitches. Complete area (4) all around center design area. Next, complete areas (2) and (3), which must align with area (4). Work area (7), same as area (1); area (8), same as area (3); area (9), same as area (1); area (10), as area (2); area (11), as area (1). Work area (12) with fly, pattern II, across top from left to right. Work fly, pattern II, also in areas (13), (14), (15). Consult outline to see where these areas begin and end. Work two rows of continental or basketweave all around design, area (16).

Colors	Craft Persian yarn color #	# of 32″ strands used
1. blue purple	87	47
2. tomato red	26	90
3. purple	93	77
4. turquoise	782	90

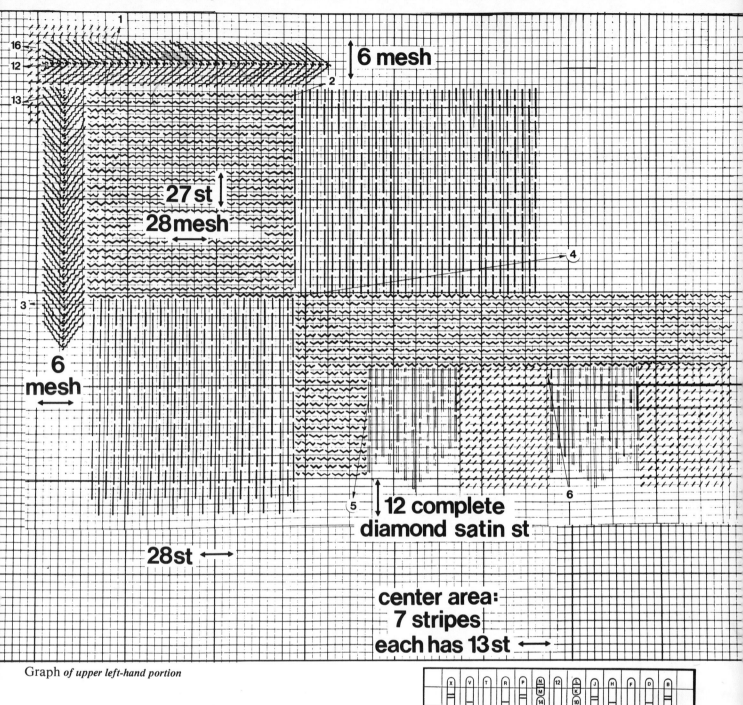

6 mesh

1

16

12

2

13

27 st
28 mesh

4

3

6 mesh

12 complete diamond satin st

5

6

28st →

center area: 7 stripes each has 13 st →

Graph *of upper left-hand portion*

Right: Diamond satin, 2-4-6-8-6-4-2 vertical pattern, for turquoise bars in center design area (photo, below)

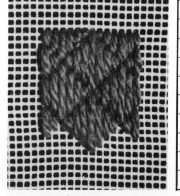

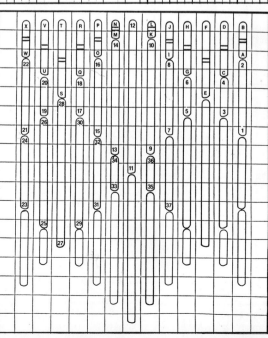

Shadows

In color, see page 34.

Diamonds made up of brilliant colors set against a black background look like tops spinning in the dark.

Circled numbers indicate order in which to work areas of canvas.
Letters indicate stitches with which to work areas of canvas.
Uncircled numbers indicate colors with which to work areas of canvas.

Outline

Work needlepoint on a piece of 22 1/4″ x 25″ #12 mono interlocked canvas. Approximate size of finished needlepoint is 16 1/4″ x 19″.

Stitches

A. Gobelin, vertical and horizontal patterns
B. continental or basketweave
C. small brick, pattern II
D. continental or basketweave
E. upright Gobelin (for multicolored diamonds)
F. Gobelin, vertical and horizontal patterns (for black diamonds)

Suggested method of working this pattern

For all stitches use the complete three-ply strand, except for the continental or basketweave which requires two plies. Starting in the upper right-hand corner of area (1), work upright Gobelin over 3 mesh across for 3 inches (overleaf right below). Then work Gobelin horizontally down the right side for 3 inches. Work area (2) with small brick, pattern II (below), across the top for 3 inches and then down right side for 3 inches. Area (3) is begun in the corner defined by small brick, pattern II, as arrow directs on graph. Using continental or basketweave, work across top of this area for 3 inches and down right side for 3 inches. You can now begin the center design area made up of areas (4) and (5). Study color chart and list (overleaf). Work the top row of multicolored diamonds (opposite below), area (4). Begin area (5) by filling in black triangles (overleaf left). Complete center design area. Complete areas (3), (2), (1). Area (6) is continental stitches on all four sides.

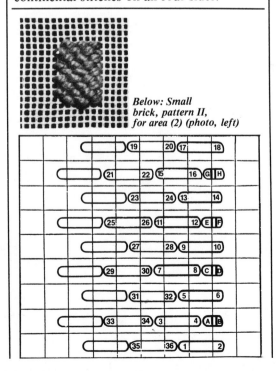

Below: Small brick, pattern II, for area (2) (photo, left)

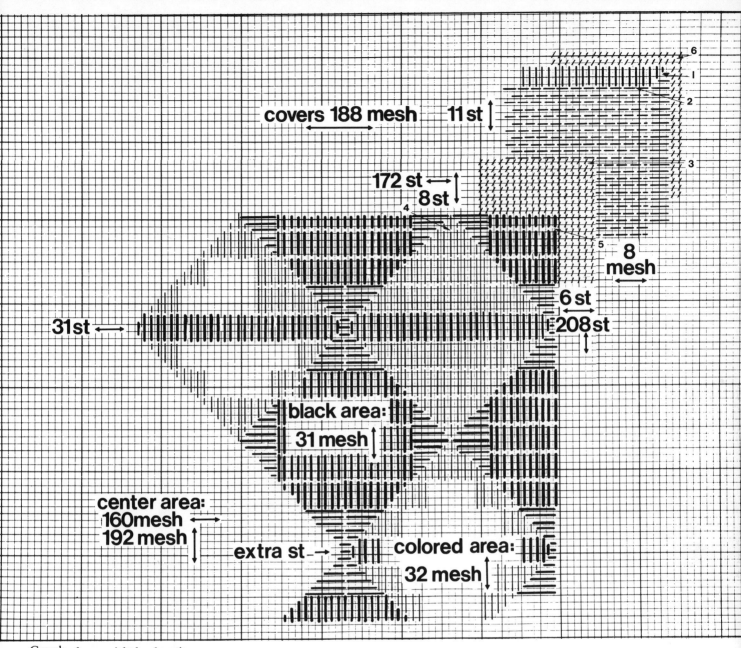

covers 188 mesh 11 st

6

1

2

3

172 st 8 st

4

5

8 mesh

6 st

31 st

208 st

black area:
31 mesh

center area:
160 mesh
192 mesh

extra st →

colored area:
32 mesh

Graph *of upper right-hand portion*

*Right: Upright Gobelin
for multicolored
diamonds of center
design area (photo, below)*

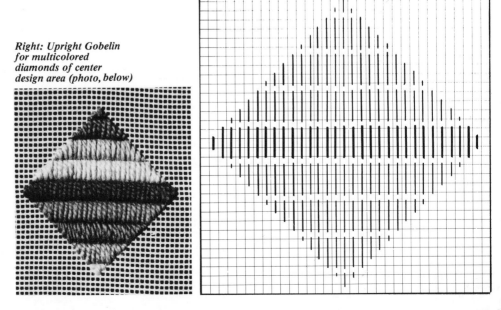

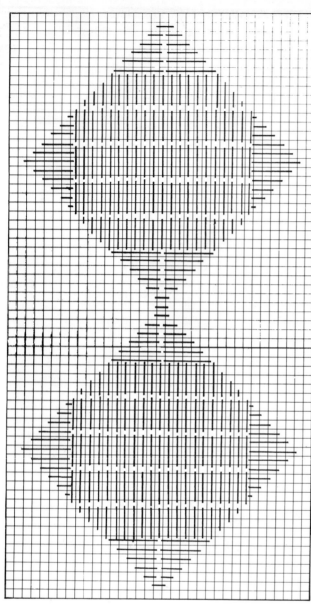

Colors	Craft Persian yarn color #	# of 32" strands used
1. rust	37	7
2. light gold	45	9
3. dark gold	46	4
4. old bronze	47	10
5. navy	95	6
6. black	96	175
7. light gray	99	4
8. ecru	103	7
9. wheat	104	3
10. coffee	105	3
11. earth	106	3
12. dark olive	112	6
13. olive	113	11
14. celadon	114	39
15. plum	125	8
16. magenta	128	9
17. old rose	129	9
18. rose pink	130	4
19. pale rose	131	4
20. dark slate blue	133	10
21. med. slate blue	134	3
22. light slate blue	135	5
23. pale blue gray	136	7
24. pink beige	139	4
25. bisque	140	4

Left: Gobelin in solid black for diamonds in center design area (photo, right)

Below: Tip of black diamonds in center design area

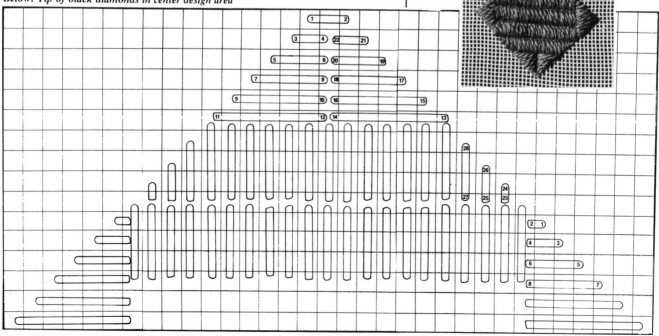

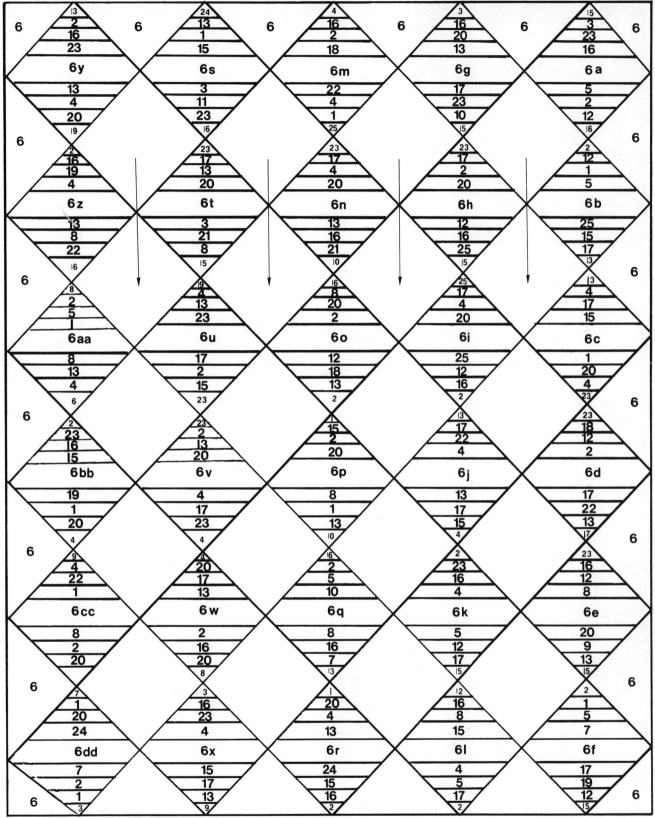

Color Chart *for center design area*

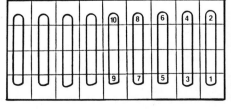

Photo and diagram (left): Upright Gobelin over 3 mesh for top and bottom of area (1); work Gobelin horizontally at sides of area (1)

55

Sunshine and Shadow

In color, see page 35.

Also known as Trip Around the World, this classic design has an almost op-art or psychedelic effect.

Work needlepoint on a piece of 17½″ x 17½″ #12 mono interlocked canvas. Approximate size of finished needlepoint is 11½″ x 11½″.

Circled numbers indicate order in which to work areas of canvas.
Letters indicate stitches with which to work areas of canvas.
Uncircled numbers indicate colors with which to work areas of canvas.

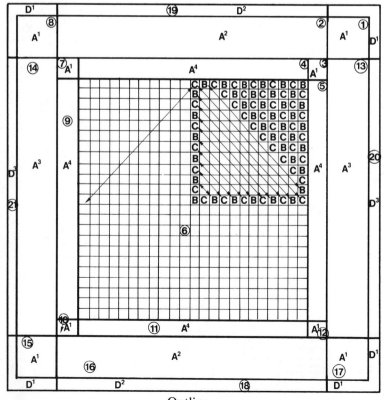

Outline

Stitches

A. small brick, pattern II
B. Scotch
C. basketweave
D. continental

Suggested method of working this pattern

For all stitches in this pattern, including the continental and basketweave, use the complete three-ply strand. Reduce the yarn to two plies for continental and basketweave if you find the yarn is too thick to move through the canvas easily. Starting in the upper right corner, area (1), work small brick, pattern II. Work area (2) across from right to left side. Work area (3), beginning where areas (1) and (2) meet. Work area (4) across for 1 inch. Work area (5) down the right side for 1 inch. Start area (6) where areas (3), (4), and (5) meet. Complete center design area, noting colors on the color chart (opposite below left) and stitches on the graph (opposite top) and special diagram (opposite below right). Complete areas (4) and (5). Work area (7), same as area (3). Area (8) repeats area (1). Work areas (9), (10), (11), and (12) around the center design, area (6). Following the outline and graph, work areas (13) and (14), areas (15) and (17), area (16). Work an outer edging of two rows of continental in areas (18), (19), (20), and (21). Note on graph that side stitches slant inward. To work them easily, turn canvas on its side.

Colors for border areas	Craft Persian yarn color #	# of 32″ strands used
1. light pink	21	29
2. pale blue	83	50
3. blue	85	50
4. medium green	73	25
Colors for area (6)		
1. light pink	21	2
4. medium green	73	6
5. light green	66	6
6. baby blue	824	6
7. deep clover	7	6
8. purple	93	6
9. medium mauve	3	6
10. light mauve	4	6
11. peach	23	6
12. apricot	24	6
13. pomegranate	27	3
14. forest green	74	6
15. tomato red	26	6

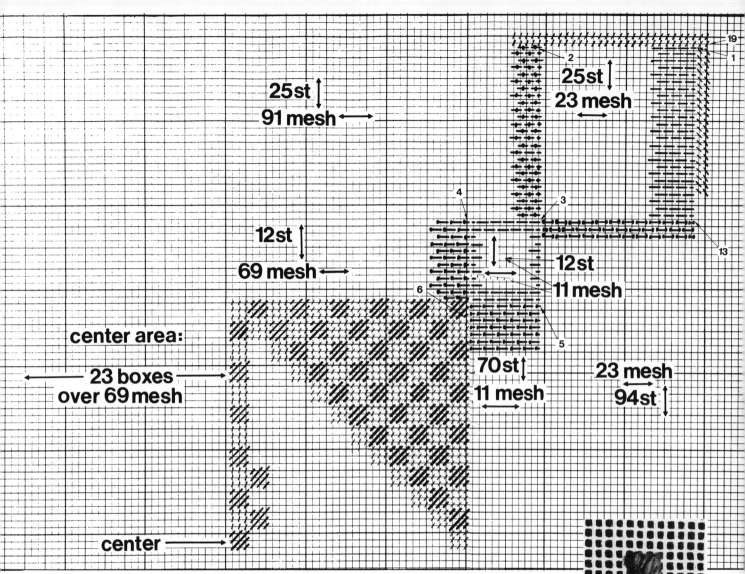

25st ↕ / 91 mesh →

25st ↕ / 23 mesh →

19
1

2

3

4

13

12st ↕ / 69 mesh →

12st ↕ / 11 mesh →

5

6

center area:

23 boxes over 69 mesh ←

center →

70st ↕ / 11 mesh →

23 mesh → / 94st ↕

Graph *of upper right quarter*

Photo *(right): Scotch over 3 mesh*

Photo and diagram (below): Scotch over 3 mesh and basketweave for center area (6)

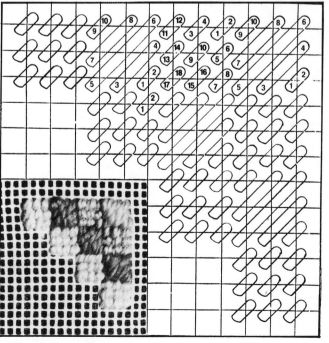

Color Chart *for area (6)*

11	13	14	5	14	6	7	8	9	10	11	12	11	10	9	8	7	6	14	5	14	13	11
13	14	5	14	6	7	8	9	10	11	12	15	12	11	10	9	8	7	6	14	5	14	13
14	5	14	6	7	8	9	10	11	12	15	14	15	12	11	10	9	8	7	6	14	5	14
5	14	6	7	8	9	10	11	12	15	14	4	14	15	12	11	10	9	8	7	6	14	5
14	6	7	8	9	10	11	12	15	14	4	5	4	14	15	12	11	10	9	8	7	6	14
6	7	8	9	10	11	12	15	14	4	5	6	5	4	14	15	12	11	10	9	8	7	6
7	8	9	10	11	12	15	14	4	5	6	7	6	5	4	14	15	12	11	10	9	8	7
8	9	10	11	12	15	14	4	5	6	7	8	7	6	5	4	14	15	12	11	10	9	8
9	10	11	12	15	14	4	5	6	7	8	9	8	7	6	5	4	14	15	12	11	10	9
10	11	12	15	14	4	5	6	7	8	9	10	9	8	7	6	5	4	14	15	12	11	10
11	12	15	14	4	5	6	7	8	9	10	1	10	9	8	7	6	5	4	14	15	12	11
12	15	14	4	5	6	7	8	9	10	1	10	1	10	9	8	7	6	5	4	14	15	12
11	12	15	14	4	5	6	7	8	9	10	1	10	9	8	7	6	5	4	14	15	12	11
10	11	12	15	14	4	5	6	7	8	9	10	9	8	7	6	5	4	14	15	12	11	10
9	10	11	12	15	14	4	5	6	7	8	9	8	7	6	5	4	14	15	12	11	10	9
8	9	10	11	12	15	14	4	5	6	7	8	7	6	5	4	14	15	12	11	10	9	8
7	8	9	10	11	12	15	14	4	5	6	7	6	5	4	14	15	12	11	10	9	8	7
6	7	8	9	10	11	12	15	14	4	5	6	5	4	14	15	12	11	10	9	8	7	6
14	6	7	8	9	10	11	12	15	14	4	5	4	14	15	12	11	10	9	8	7	6	14
5	14	6	7	8	9	10	11	12	15	14	4	14	15	12	11	10	9	8	7	6	14	5
14	5	14	6	7	8	9	10	11	12	15	14	15	12	11	10	9	8	7	6	14	5	14
13	14	5	14	6	7	8	9	10	11	12	15	12	11	10	9	8	7	6	14	5	14	13
11	13	14	5	14	6	7	8	9	10	11	12	11	10	9	8	7	6	14	5	14	13	11

2
9
10 8 6 12 4 2 10 8 6
11 3 1 9
4 14 10 6 4
7 13 9 5 7
2 18 16 8 2
5 3 1 17 15 7 5 3 1
2
1

Rainbow
In color, see page 35.

Made by a Pennsylvania German, this non-Amish design reveals the strong influence the Amish had on their neighbors.

Work the needlepoint on a piece of 19″ x 18½″ #12 mono interlocked canvas. Approximate size of finished needlepoint is 13″ x 12½″.

Circled numbers indicate order in which to work areas of canvas.
Letters indicate stitches with which to work areas of canvas.
Uncircled numbers indicate colors with which to work areas of canvas.

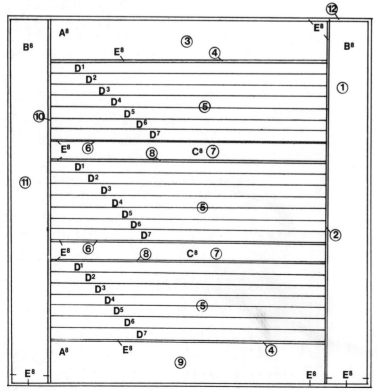

Outline

Stitches

A. small brick, pattern II
B. small brick, pattern I
C. small brick, pattern II
D. Scotch
E. continental, horizontal and vertical

Suggested method of working this pattern

All stitches, including the continental, in areas (1) through (11) require the complete strand of three-ply yarn. Area (12) uses only two plies. For area (1) use small brick, pattern I. Area (2) consists of a line of vertical continental stitches alongside area (1). Fill in area (3) with small brick, pattern II, 130 mesh across. Work area (4), a row of horizontal continental for 130 mesh. Area (5) consists of Scotch stitches over 5 mesh (opposite below right) with a total of 26 Scotch stitches in each row. There are seven rows of Scotch in each area (5). Work first row of Scotch from right to left; invert the canvas to work the next row in the opposite direction, to prevent distorting the canvas. Consult outline for placement of colors. Area (6) is the same as area (4), a row of horizontal continental. Area (7) is small brick, pattern II, 10 stitches deep. Area (8) is the same as area (4), a row of horizontal continental. Following the outline, complete the entire center design. Area (9) is the same as area (3), small brick, pattern II. Area (10) is the same as area (2), a line of vertical continental stitches. Area (11) is the same as area (1), small brick, pattern I. For area (12) work two rows of continental on all four sides using only two plies of yarn.

Colors	Craft Persian yarn color #	# of 32″ strands used
1. pink	5	29
2. poppy red	18	29
3. tangerine	25	29
4. canary yellow	486	29
5. antique bronze	54	29
6. peacock blue	79	29
7. pale gray	100	29
8. beige	122	106

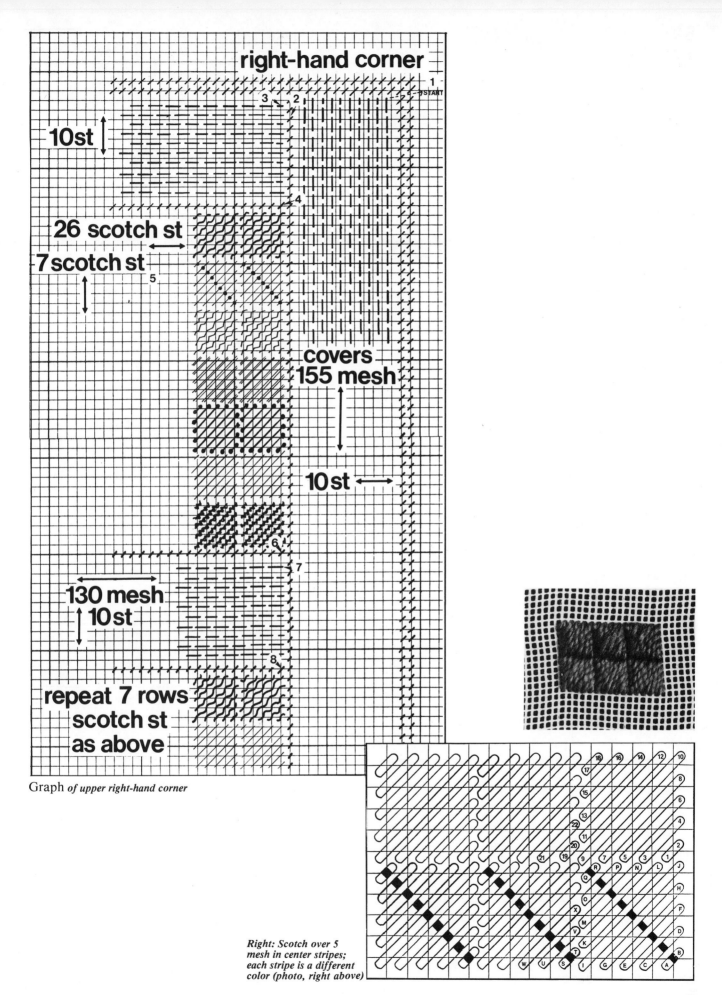

right-hand corner

10st

26 scotch st

7 scotch st

covers
155 mesh

10 st

130 mesh
10 st

repeat 7 rows
scotch st
as above

START

Graph *of upper right-hand corner*

*Right: Scotch over 5
mesh in center stripes;
each stripe is a different
color (photo, right above)*

Bars

In color, see page 35.

The use of off-white is unusual for the Amish in an otherwise traditional Bars quilt.

Work the needlepoint on a piece of 21″ x 20¾″ #13 mono interlocked canvas. Approximate size of finished needlepoint is 15″ x 14¾″.

Circled numbers indicate order in which to work areas of canvas.
Letters indicate stitches with which to work areas of canvas.
Uncircled numbers indicate colors with which to work areas of canvas.

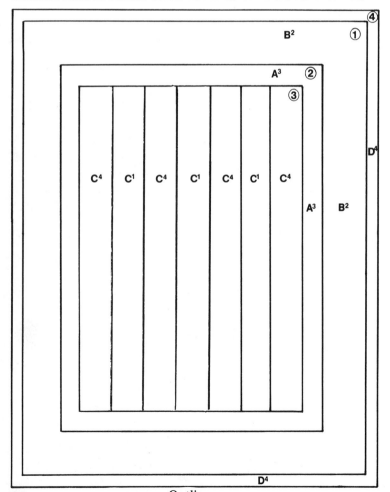

Outline

Stitches

A. upright Gobelin in diagonal progression
B. upright Gobelin (ridge design)
C. diamond satin, 2-4-6-8-6-4-2 vertical pattern
D. continental or basketweave

Suggested method of working this pattern

For all stitches use the complete three-ply strand, except for the continental or basketweave which requires two plies. Area (1) is begun in the upper right-hand corner where arrow directs on graph. Work across the top and down the right side for 4 inches using the upright Gobelin in a ridge (below and opposite below center). Do not complete area (1) yet. Start area (2). Use the upright Gobelin in diagonal progression over 4 mesh (photo and diagram, opposite top left). Again, work across the top and down the right side for 4 inches only. Area (3) is the center design area. It consists of seven bars 2-4-6-8-6-4-2 vertical diamond satin. Return to area (2), continue Gobelin in diagonal progression all around center design. Note placement of stitches in corners (see graphs, opposite below). Complete area (1), which surrounds area (2). Work two rows of continental on all four sides, area (4).

Colors	Craft Persian yarn color #	# of 32″ strands used
1. olive	113	85
2. med. slate blue	134	119
3. off-white	102	60
4. light violet	91	67

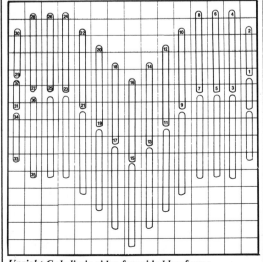

Upright Gobelin in ridge for wide blue frame (photo, opposite below center)

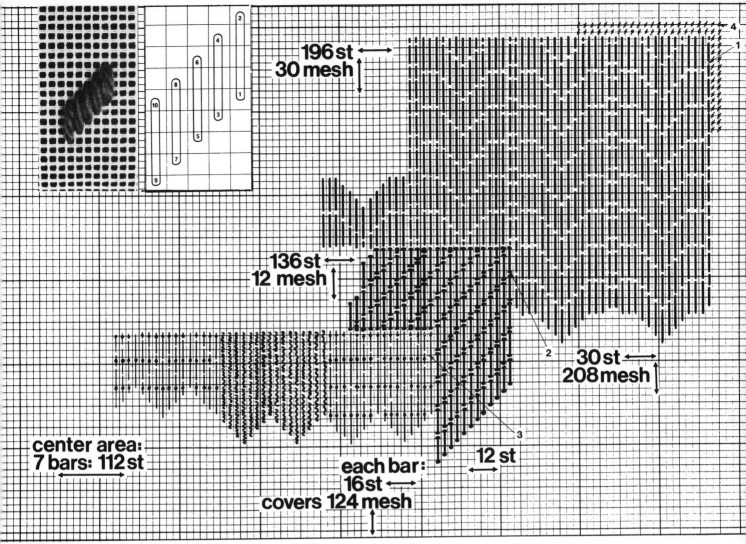

196 st
30 mesh

136 st
12 mesh

30 st
208 mesh

center area:
7 bars: 112 st

each bar:
16 st
covers 124 mesh

12 st

Graph *of upper right-hand portion*

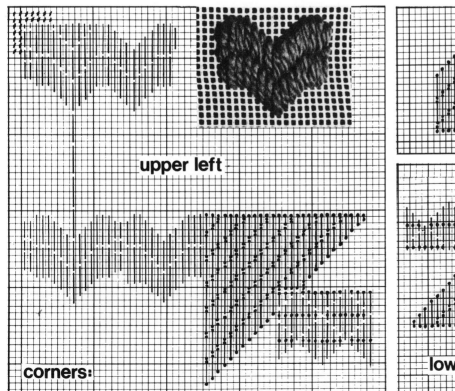

upper left

corners:

Photo and diagram (upper left-hand corner):
Upright Gobelin in diagonal progression for area (2)

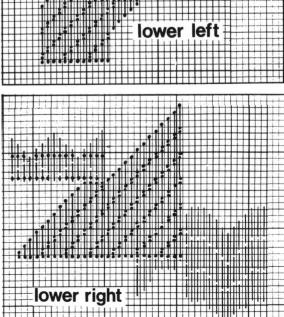

lower left

lower right

Above: Graphs of corners in area (2)

61

Courthouse Steps

In color, see page 36.

This Courthouse Steps variation of a Log Cabin design consists of a dramatic center of magenta, mustard, black.

Work the needlepoint on a piece of 22″ x 23″ #12 mono interlocked canvas. Approximate size of finished needlepoint is 16″ x 17″.

Circled numbers indicate order in which to work areas of canvas.
Letters indicate stitches with which to work areas of canvas.
Uncircled numbers indicate colors with which to work areas of canvas.

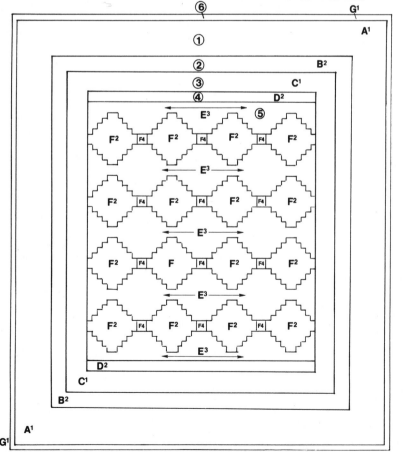

Outline

Stitches

A. diamond satin, 2-4-6-8-6-4-2 vertical pattern
B. Parisian
C. diamond satin, 2-4-6-8-6-4-2 vertical pattern
D. large brick, pattern II
E. upright Gobelin
F. Gobelin, horizontal pattern
G. continental or basketweave

Suggested method of working this pattern

For all stitches use the complete three-ply strand, except for the continental or basketweave which requires two plies. Starting at the upper right corner, work area (1), 24 diamond satin patterns wide across the top, and then down the right side to a depth of 26 diamond satin patterns. Work area (2) in Parisian across the top for 6 inches and down the right side for 6 inches. Area (3) consists of more diamond satin patterns. Work them across the top for 5 inches. Work area (4) with large brick, pattern II, as shown on graph. Now begin the center design, area (5). Starting where arrow directs on the graph, use E^3 (upright Gobelin in mustard). Work the area across the top (see outline). Next work a row of F^2 patterns (Gobelin, horizontally, in magenta) and F^4 patterns (Gobelin, horizontally, in black). Complete center in this manner, from the top down. Below area (5) work large brick, pattern II, as in area (4). Complete area (3) around center; complete area (2). Finish area (1). Work two rows continental all around, area (6).

Colors	Craft Persian yarn color #	# of 32″ strands used
1. beige	122	150
2. magenta	128	90
3. mustard	408	45
4. black	96	10

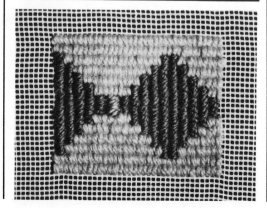

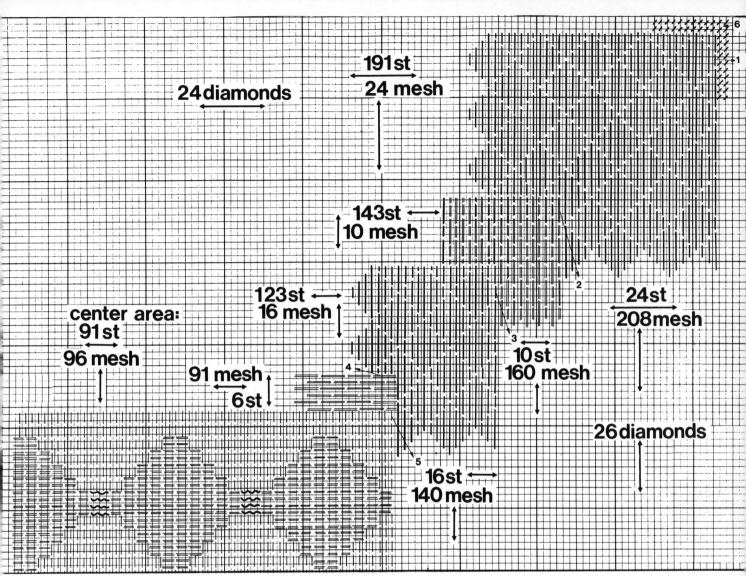

24 diamonds

191 st / 24 mesh

143 st / 10 mesh

123 st / 16 mesh

center area: / 91 st / 96 mesh

91 mesh / 6 st

24 st / 208 mesh

10 st / 160 mesh

26 diamonds

16 st / 140 mesh

Graph *of upper right-hand portion*

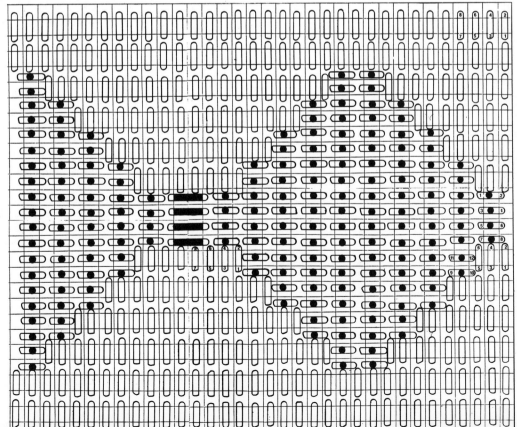

Photo and diagram (opposite below right and right): Gobelin over 2 mesh, vertical and horizontal patterns, in center design area

Bars

In color, see page 36.

The traditional Bars pattern
has an unusual boldness
and purity with its
tricolors of blue, red, and ecru.

Work needlepoint on a piece of 20½″ x 20½″ #12 mono interlocked canvas. Approximate size of finished needlepoint is 14½″ x 14½″.

Circled numbers indicate order in which to work areas of canvas.
Letters indicate stitches with which to work areas of canvas.
Uncircled numbers indicate colors with which to work areas of canvas.

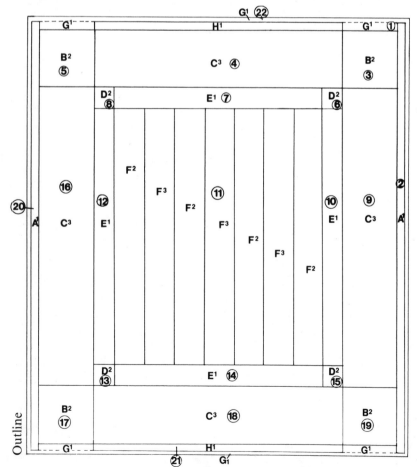

Outline

Stitches

A. small brick, pattern I
B. large brick, pattern I
C. large brick, pattern II
D. large brick, pattern I
E. continental or basketweave
F. diamond satin, 2-4-6-8-6-4-2 vertical
   pattern
G. continental
H. small brick, pattern II

Suggested method of working this pattern

For all stitches use the complete three-ply strand, except for the continental or basketweave which requires two plies. Area (1) is begun in the top right corner; arrow on graph (opposite above) directs you to the place. Using the continental, work across top for 24 stitches. Then work small brick, pattern II, for 4 inches. For area (2) work down right side for 4 inches using small brick, pattern I. Now work area (3) with large brick, pattern I. Work area (4) using large brick, pattern II. Area (5) is the same as area (3). In area (6) use large brick, pattern I. Work the continental or basketweave across in area (7). Area (8) repeats area (6). In area (9) work large brick, pattern II, down right side for 4 inches. Area (10) is continental or basketweave. Now you are ready to begin the center portion of needlepoint, area (11). Work center in diamond satin, 2-4-6-8-6-4-2 vertical pattern (opposite below), following the outline for color changes. There are seven vertical bars in area (11). Area (12) repeats area (10). Area (13) repeats area (8). Area (14) repeats area (7). Area (15) repeats area (6). Now complete area (9). Area (16) repeats area (9). Area (17) repeats area (5). Area (18) repeats area (4). Area (19) repeats area (3). Complete area (1) with three rows of 24 continental stitches above area (5); the remainder of the area is filled in with small brick, pattern II. Area (21) is worked as area (1): continental below areas (19) and (17) and small brick, pattern II, under area (18). Now complete area (2) and work area (20) to correspond. Finally, work two rows of continental stitches on all four sides for area (22).

Colors	Craft Persian yarn color #	# of 32″ strands used
1. blueberry	86	30
2. poppy red	18	50
3. ecru	103	85

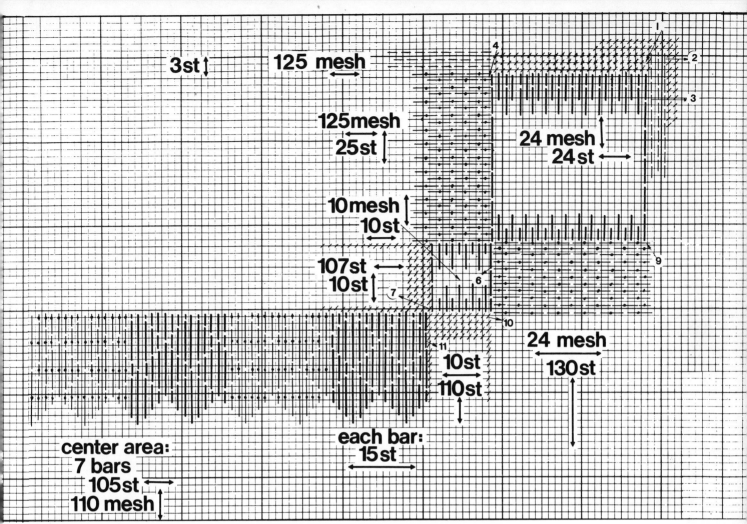

3st

125 mesh

125mesh
25st

24 mesh
24 st

10mesh
10st

107st
10st

6

7

9

10

11

10st
110st

24 mesh
130st

each bar:
15st

center area:
7 bars
105st
110 mesh

Graph *of upper right-hand portion*

Right: Diamond satin,
2-4-6-8-6-4-2 vertical pattern,
for bars in center design area
(photo, below)

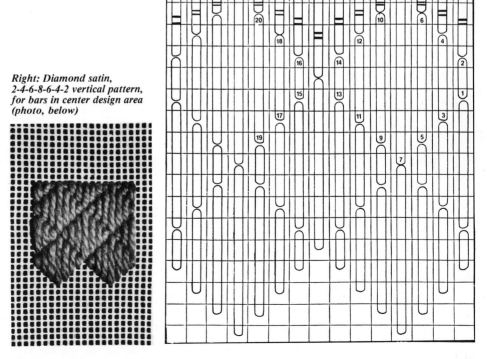

Diamond

In color, see pages 36–37.

Eight rosebud stitches and a border of diamond satins give this needlework a three-dimensional look.

Work the needlepoint on a piece of 20" x 19¾" #12 mono interlocked canvas. Approximate size of finished needlepoint is 14" x 13¾".

Circled numbers indicate order in which to work areas of canvas.
Letters indicate stitches with which to work areas of canvas.
Uncircled numbers indicate colors with which to work areas of canvas.

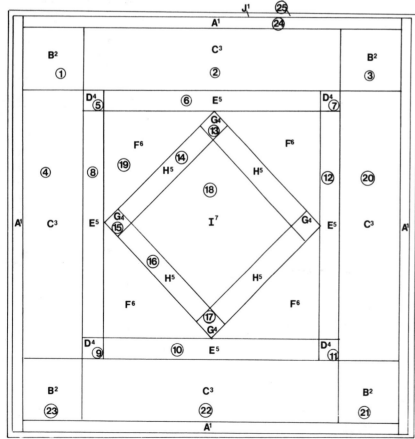

Outline

Stitches

A. Gobelin, vertical and horizontal patterns
B. large brick, pattern II
C. diamond satin, 2-4-6-8-6-4-2 vertical pattern
D. rosebud (over 8 mesh)
E. continental or basketweave
F. small brick, pattern II
G. diagonal rosebud (over 12 mesh)
H. continental or basketweave
I. Parisian
J. continental

Suggested method of working this pattern

For all stitches use the complete three-ply strand, except for the continental or basketweave which requires two plies. Work area (1) with large brick, pattern II. Next work area (2) to a width of 15 diamond satins in 2-4-6-8-6-4-2 vertical pattern. Area (3) is same as area (1). For area (4) work diamond satins down left side for 4 inches (see graph). Area (5) is a rosebud over 8 mesh with continental around (opposite below center). Work area (6) in continental, 98 mesh wide. Work area (7) same as area (5). Work area (8) in continental. Area (9) is same as area (5); area (10), same as area (6); area (11), same as area (5); area (12), same as area (8). With sewing thread make an outline of diamond (drawing, opposite below left). Starting in the 50th space on the top row of unworked center square, work a diagonal rosebud over 12 mesh (opposite below right) for area (13). Area (14) is worked in continental or basketweave. Area (15) is another diagonal rosebud, cornered in the 50th space down left side of center square. Area (16) is same as area (14). Area (17) corresponds to area (13). Work area (18) in Parisian. Complete diamond at center. Work the triangles of area (19). Complete area (4). Area (21) is same as area (1); area (22), same as area (2); area (23), same as area (1). For area (24) work Gobelin over 3 mesh. Area (25) is two rows continental all around.

Colors	Craft Persian yarn color #	# of 32" strands used
1. strawberry	10	25
2. plum	125	20
3. light plum	126	80
4. purple	93	13
5. medium green	73	40
6. sea blue	84	42
7. rhubarb	16	40

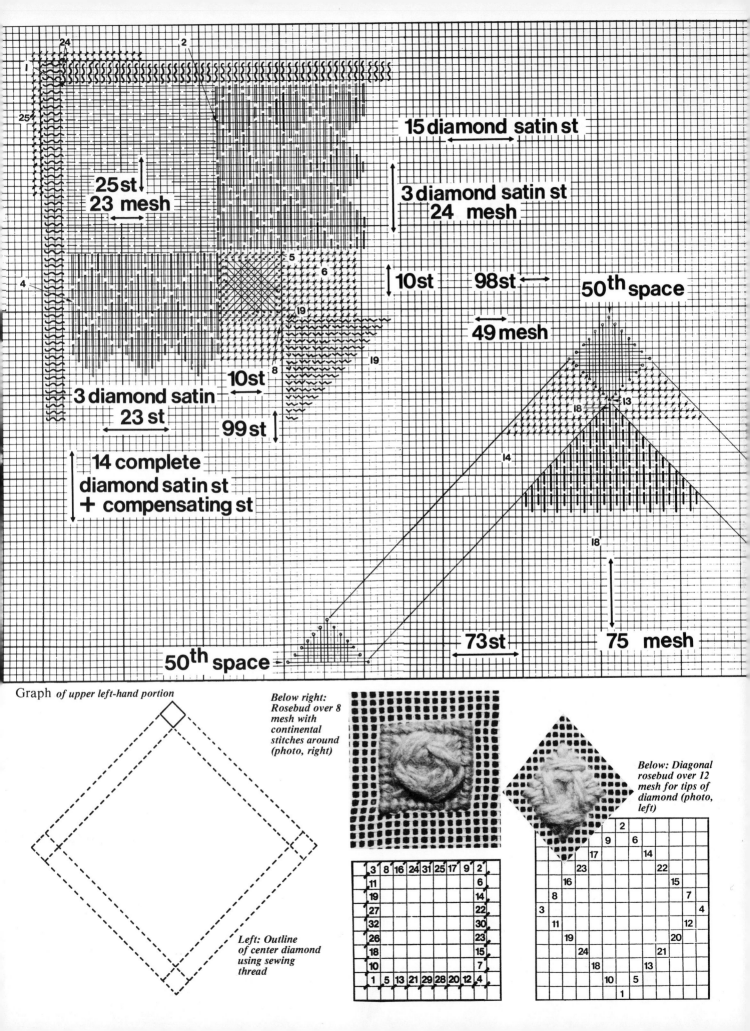

15 diamond satin st

25 st
23 mesh

3 diamond satin st
24 mesh

10 st

98 st

50th space

49 mesh

10 st

3 diamond satin
23 st

99 st

14 complete
diamond satin st
+ compensating st

18

13

14

18

50th space

73 st

75 mesh

Graph *of upper left-hand portion*

*Below right:
Rosebud over 8
mesh with
continental
stitches around
(photo, right)*

*Below: Diagonal
rosebud over 12
mesh for tips of
diamond (photo,
left)*

*Left: Outline
of center diamond
using sewing
thread*

3	8	16	24	31	25	17	9	2
11								6
19								14
27								22
32								30
26								23
18								15
10								7
1	5	13	21	29	28	20	12	4

					2		
				9		6	
			17		14		
		23				22	
	16						15
8							7
3							4
11							12
19						20	
24					21		
18				13			
10		5					
1							

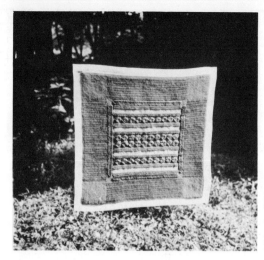

Split Bars

In color, see page 38.

The different textures of the bars in the center of this needlepoint make it resemble a well-kept garden patch.

Work the needlepoint on a piece of 20" x 20" #12 mono interlocked canvas. Approximate size of finished needlepoint is 14" x 14".

Circled numbers indicate order in which to work areas of canvas.
Letters indicate stitches with which to work areas of canvas.
Uncircled numbers indicate colors with which to work areas of canvas.

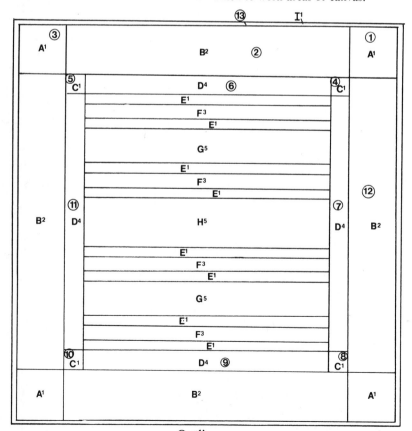

Outline

Stitches

A. small brick, pattern II
B. Parisian
C. continental or basketweave
D. fly, pattern II
E. fly, pattern I
F. continental or basketweave
G. rosebud (over 9 mesh)
H. rosebud (over 9 mesh)
I. continental or basketweave

Suggested method of working this pattern

For all stitches use the complete three-ply strand, except for the continental or basketweave which requires two plies. Area (1) is begun in upper right-hand corner. Use small brick, pattern II. Work Parisian stitch in area (2). Work area (3) with small brick, pattern II. Area (4) is a square of continental. Work area (5) like area (4). Stitch a row of continental from area (4) to area (5), just under area (2), to begin center design, area (6).

Work fly, pattern II, from right to left first. Then add a row of horizontal continental below fly. Work the bars in the center: 6E, fly, pattern I (opposite below right); 6F, continental or basketweave; 6G, rosebud over 9 mesh (opposite below left), framed by a row of continental. Work these rows in the order shown on outline. 6H is the middle of the center design: two rows of rosebud over 9 mesh, framed by a row of continental. Work lower portion of center design same as top (see outline). Begin area (7) by stitching a row of vertical continental along right side of center design area. Work fly, pattern II, down right side. Add a row of vertical continental on other side of fly. Area (8) is same as area (4). Area (9) is same as area (6): fly, pattern II, plus continental above and below. Area (10) is same as area (5). Area (11) repeats area (7): fly, pattern II, bordered by continental. For area (12) work Parisian down right side. Work it down left side under area (3). Work bottom of canvas as top areas (1), (2), (3). Work area (13) with two rows of continental all around.

Colors	Craft Persian yarn color #	# of 32" strands used
1. poppy red	18	68
2. cranberry	9	72
3. hot pink	6	17
4. royal blue	855	27
5. green	65	44

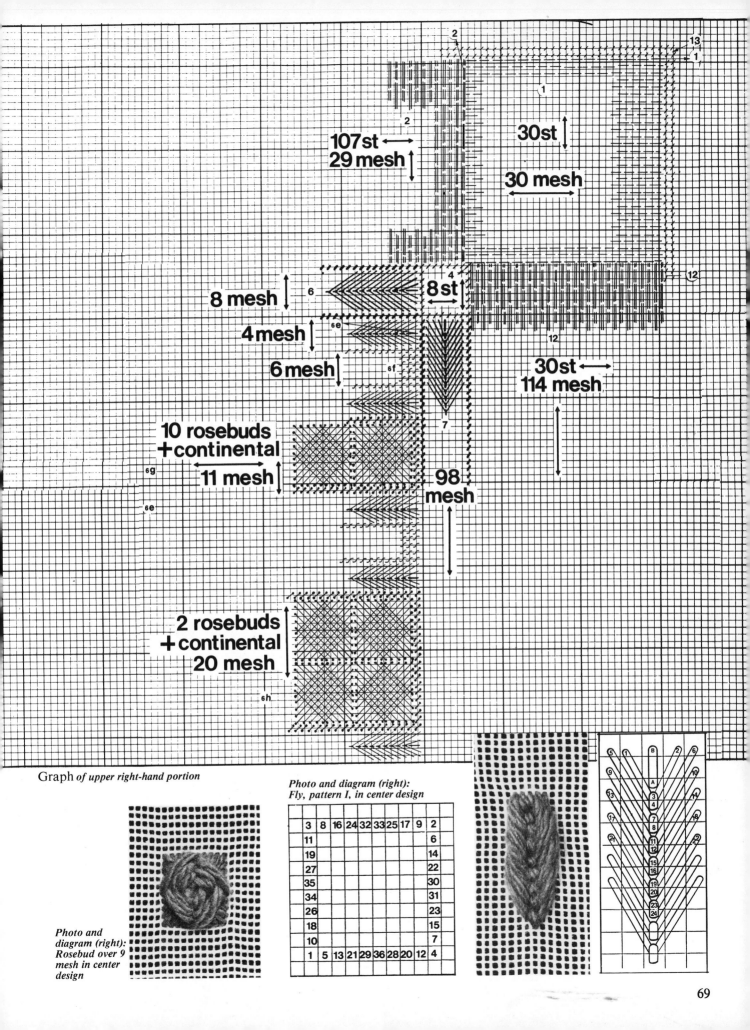

107st ←→
29 mesh ↕

30st ↕

30 mesh ←→

8 mesh ↕   6 ←   8 st ←→

4 mesh ↕   6e

6 mesh ↕   6f

30st ←→
114 mesh

10 rosebuds
+continental
11 mesh ↕   6g

98
mesh

6e

2 rosebuds
+continental
20 mesh   6h

Graph *of upper right-hand portion*

*Photo and diagram (right):
Fly, pattern I, in center design*

3	8	16	24	32	33	25	17	9	2
11									6
19									14
27									22
35									30
34									31
26									23
18									15
10									7
1	5	13	21	29	36	28	20	12	4

Photo and diagram (right): Rosebud over 9 mesh in center design

Checker-board

In color, see page 38.

The three-dimensionality of the flowers makes them stand out from their backgrounds of the same colors.

Work needlepoint on a piece of 19¼″ x 21¾″ #13 mono interlocked canvas. Approximate size of finished needlepoint is 13¼″ x 15¾″.

Circled numbers indicate order in which to work areas of canvas.
Letters indicate stitches with which to work areas of canvas.
Uncircled numbers indicate colors with which to work areas of canvas.

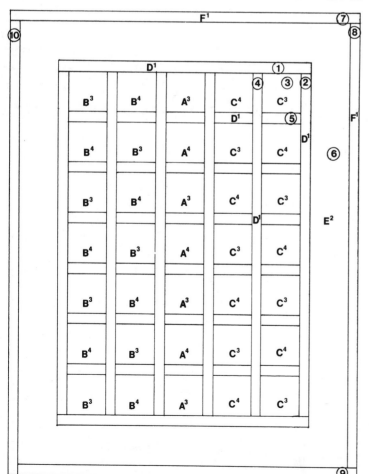

Outline

Stitches

A. Gobelin (upright flower)
B. Gobelin (flower facing right)
C. Gobelin (flower facing left)
D. Gobelin (ovals)
E. Gobelin (flowers in border)
F. continental or basketweave

Suggested method of working this pattern

For all stitches use the complete three-ply strand, except for the continental or basketweave which requires two plies. Special note: Most of the stitches in this needlepoint are Gobelin, but they are grouped in different directions to form flowers and ovals. On outline (left below): A is a horizontal pattern for an upright flower; B is in different directions to form a flower facing right; C is in different directions to form a flower facing left; D is in a small oval, pattern II (overleaf right). Start at area (1). Work 12 ovals in upright Gobelin across top. Then work oval patterns down side, area (2), for 4 inches. Here use Gobelin in horizontal pattern. Consult graph (opposite top), special graph on overleaf left, and diagrams on overleaf right for proper positioning of flowers in center boxes. Work first flower facing left (C) in box labeled area (3). Surround flower with continental or basketweave. Begin area (4), stripes running down center. Again use Gobelin, horizontal pattern, in oval patterns and again fill in around them with continental or basketweave. Work only 6 ovals. Following graph and outline, work across first row of boxes and stripes. Work area (5), first of horizontal stripes. Note: There is 1 stitch less between ovals in area (5) horizontal stripes than between ovals in areas (1), (2), and (4). Work flowers in second row of boxes. Repeat area (5) below boxes. Lengthen areas (2) and (4). Each vertical stripe will have 16 ovals when you complete center design area. Work area (6), flower border. Turn special graph (overleaf left) upside down for placement of flowers in left and bottom border. In areas (7), (8), (9), and (10) work continental or basketweave all around.

Colors	Craft Persian yarn color #	# of 32″ strands used
1. loden	64	60
2. blueberry	86	80
3. burgundy	17	80
4. dark purple	94	80

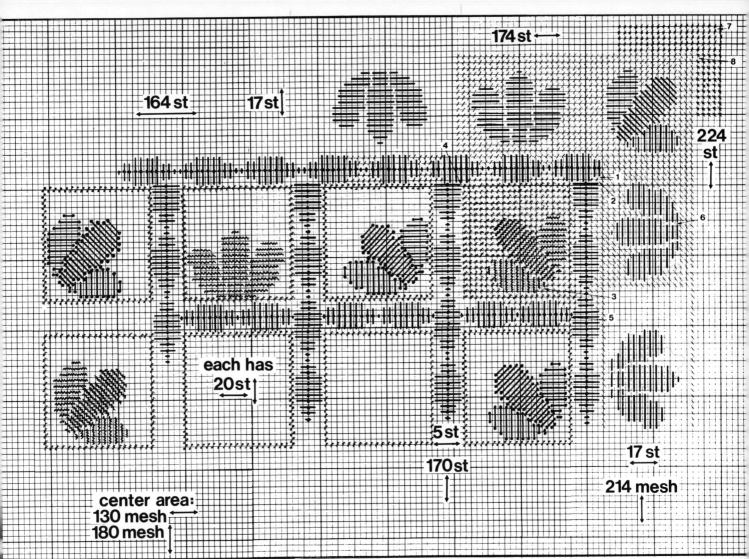

164 st

17 st

174 st →

224 st

each has 20 st

5 st

170 st

center area:
130 mesh
180 mesh

17 st

214 mesh

Graph *of upper portion*

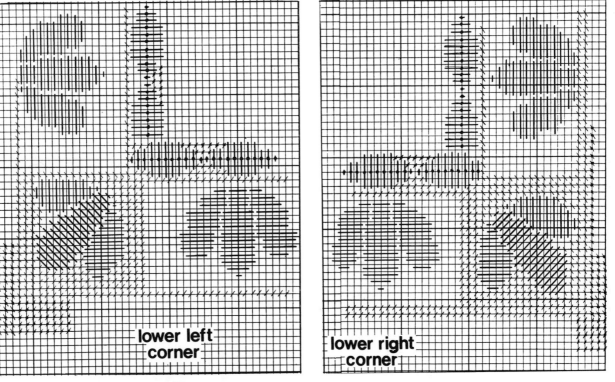

lower left corner

lower right corner

Above: Corners showing placement of flowers in border area

Special graph for placement of boxed flowers, border flowers, and ovals

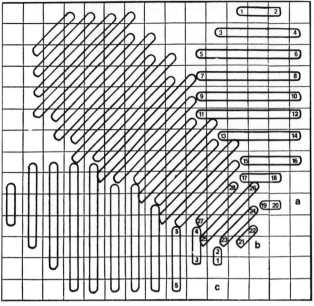

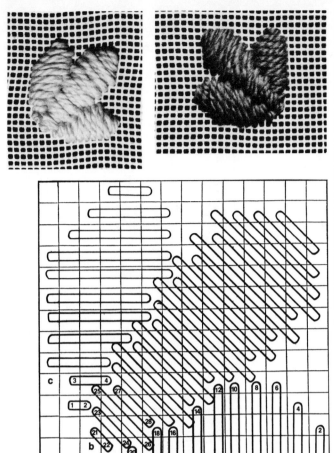

Above: Gobelin for flower facing left (photo, above left)

Above: Gobelin for flower facing right (photo, top left)

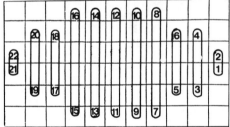

Photo and diagram (above): Upright Gobelin in small oval, pattern II, for areas (1) and (5); use pattern horizontally for areas (2) and (4)

Below: Gobelin for upright flower (photo, below right)

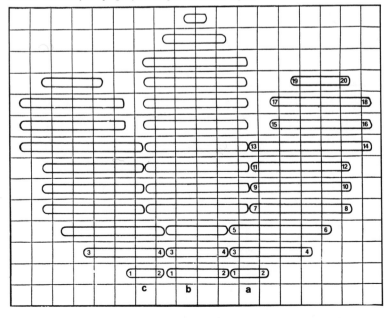

73

Single Irish Chain

In color, see page 38.

The design is concentrated in a large center motif, shimmering chains of rose against a black background.

Work needlepoint on a piece of 23⅜″ x 26⅜″ #12 mono interlocked canvas. Approximate size of finished needlepoint is 17⅜″ x 20⅜″.

Circled numbers indicate order in which to work areas of canvas.
Letters indicate stitches with which to work areas of canvas.
Uncircled numbers indicate colors with which to work areas of canvas.

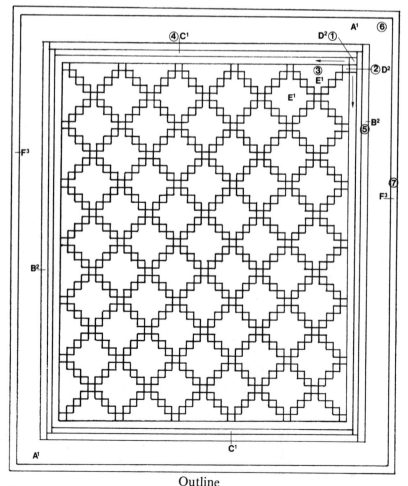

Outline

Stitches

A. upright Gobelin in diagonal progression
B. Scotch
C. Gobelin, vertical and horizontal patterns (over 3 mesh)
D. double leviathan
E. Gobelin, vertical and horizontal patterns (over 4 mesh)
F. continental or basketweave

Suggested method of working this pattern

For all stitches use four plies of yarn, except for the continental or basketweave, which requires three. Count down approximately 30 mesh from the top and about 20 mesh in from the right side of area to be worked. Bring the needle up in the space below the 30th mesh and start area (1) with a double leviathan. Then work another one directly underneath. Work a third double leviathan to the left of the second one (see graph, opposite top). This begins area (2). Work chains of double leviathan to match pattern on outline (left) and graph. Use the Gobelin over 4 mesh to fill in between the chains (opposite below left), area (3). Note: Top and bottom halves of diamonds in area (3) are worked with upright stitches while complete diamonds and side halves of diamonds use the Gobelin in horizontal direction. After completing center design area, work remaining double leviathans in a frame all around. Next surround double leviathans with a frame of upright Gobelin worked over 3 mesh, area (4). Note: Stitches run upright on top and bottom and horizontally at sides. Outline shows how far rows extend. Area (5) consists of Gobelin in each corner and then a row of Scotch over 4 mesh (opposite top left corner) between. For area (6) work upright Gobelin in diagonal progression over 4 mesh (opposite below center). See corner graphs (opposite below right). Lower left corner is upside-down version of upper right corner. Using three plies of yarn, work area (7) in continental or basketweave for at least two rows on all four sides. Here we have used four rows.

Colors	Craft Persian yarn color #	# of 32″ strands used
1. black	96	320
2. old rose	129	320
3. white	101	32

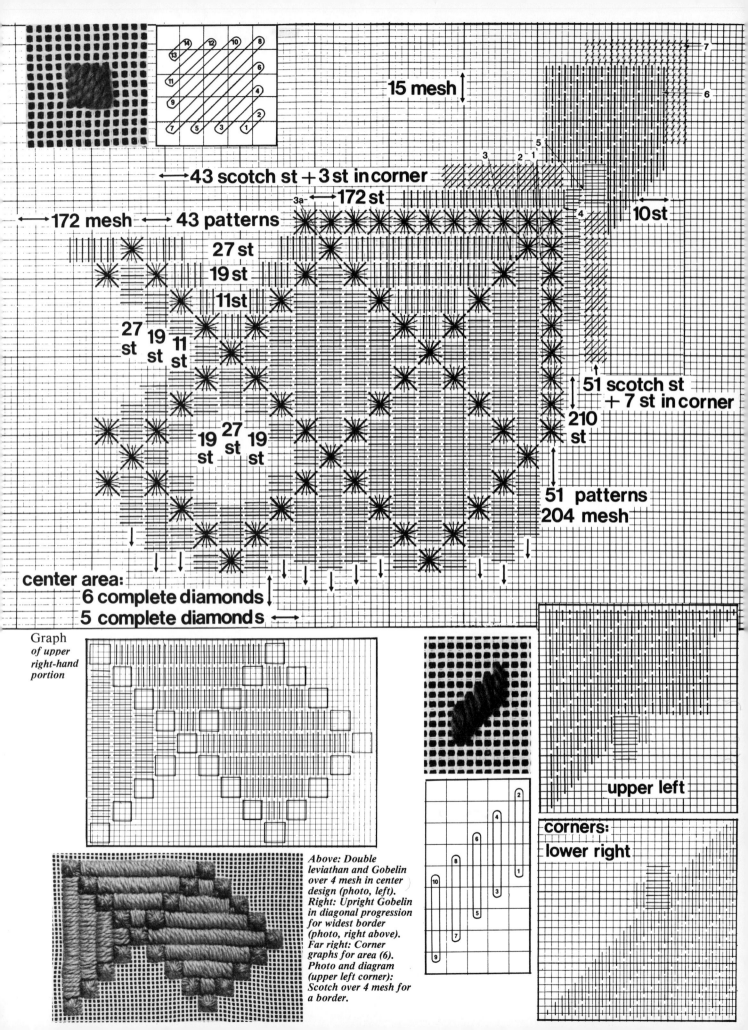

15 mesh

43 scotch st + 3 st in corner

172 st

3a ←

172 mesh ← → 43 patterns

27 st

19 st

11 st

27 19 11
st st st

19 27 19
st st st

3 2 1 5

4

10 st

51 scotch st
+ 7 st in corner

210
st

51 patterns
204 mesh

center area:
6 complete diamonds
5 complete diamonds

Graph
*of upper
right-hand
portion*

upper left

corners:
lower right

*Above: Double
leviathan and Gobelin
over 4 mesh in center
design (photo, left).
Right: Upright Gobelin
in diagonal progression
for widest border
(photo, right above).
Far right: Corner
graphs for area (6).
Photo and diagram
(upper left corner):
Scotch over 4 mesh for
a border.*

Nine-Patch

In color, see page 39.

Many shapes combine in this needlepoint: square patches at the center, ovals around it, baskets in corners.

Work needlepoint on a piece of 18¾″ x 19¼″ #12 mono interlocked canvas. Approximate size of finished needlepoint is 12¾″ x 13¼″.

Circled numbers indicate order in which to work areas of canvas.
Letters indicate stitches with which to work areas of canvas.
Uncircled numbers indicate colors with which to work areas of canvas.

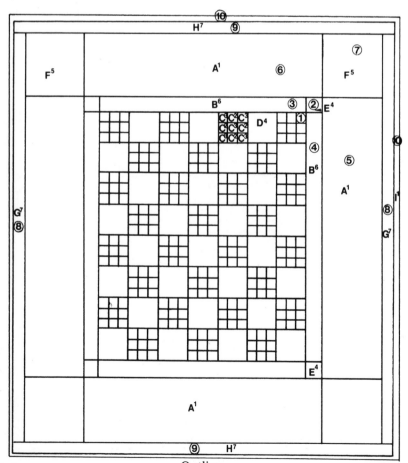

Outline

Stitches

A. diamond satin, 2-4-6-4-2 vertical pattern
B. Gobelin in oval, pattern III, plus continental
C. upright Gobelin in checkerboard
D. upright Gobelin in diagonal progression
E. raised pyramid
F. Gobelin, vertical and horizontal patterns, plus continental
G. diamond satin, 2-4-6 vertical pattern
H. upright Gobelin
I. continental or basketweave

Suggested method of working this pattern

For all stitches use the complete three-ply strand, except for the continental or basketweave which requires two plies. Count down about 39 mesh from the top and in about 39 mesh from the right side of the area to be worked on the canvas. Start area (1) where arrow directs on graph (opposite top). Work all the center's alternate boxes of upright Gobelin in checkerboard and upright Gobelin in diagonal progression (see stitch diagrams, overleaf left). For area (2) work a raised pyramid (opposite below). In area (3) work upright Gobelin in oval, pattern III (see overleaf left), across for a total of seven ovals. Use continental to fill in around ovals. Work the Gobelin horizontally in oval, pattern III, down right side of center boxes, area (4). Note: Between ovals 4 and 5 you must eliminate a stitch. Continue until there are a total of eight patterns. Fill in around ovals with continental or basketweave. Repeat raised pyramid in lower right corner, corresponding to area (2). Work ovals along bottom of center design area, corresponding to area (3). Work left side of center area same as right side: raised pyramids in corners and ovals surrounded by continental or basketweave. Work one row of vertical continental in loden from top of raised pyramid, area (2), to bottom of raised pyramid below area (4). Now work area (5) in diamond satin, 2-4-6-4-2 vertical pattern, on right side (see overleaf left). Work area (6) across top as area (5). For area (7) work a basket in upper right-hand corner using Gobelin surrounded by continental. Repeat area (5) on left side. Repeat area (6) on bottom. Work baskets in other corners. Area (8) is 2-4-6 vertical diamond satin. Area (9) is Gobelin. Work two rows continental or basketweave all around for area (10).

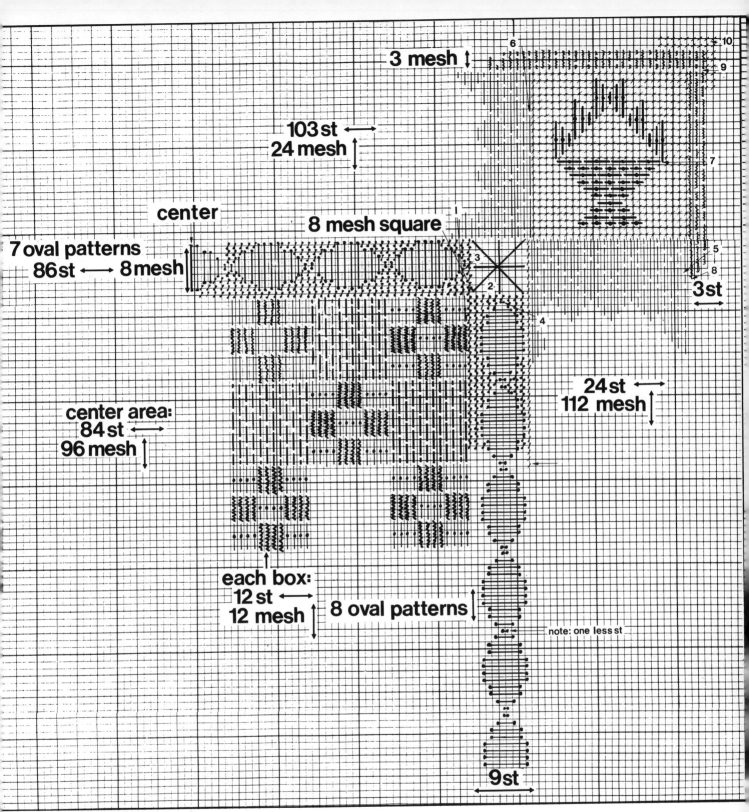

3 mesh

103 st → 24 mesh

center

8 mesh square

7 oval patterns 86 st ← → 8 mesh

3st

center area: 84 st → 96 mesh

24 st → 112 mesh

each box: 12 st ← → 12 mesh

8 oval patterns

note: one less st

9st

Graph *of upper right-hand portion*

Photo and diagram (right): Raised pyramid in four small corner blocks

	18	16	14	12	10	8	6	4	2	
20										31
22										29
24										27
26										25
28										23
30										21
32										19
1	3	5	7	9	11	13	15	17	

Colors	Craft Persian yarn color #	# of 32'' strands used
1. magenta	128	100
2. pink beige	139	25
3. cranberry	9	30
4. dark olive	112	45
5. pale mint	115	20
6. loden	64	30
7. leaf green	56	20

Below: Upright Gobelin in diagonal progression for boxes in center design (photo, left)

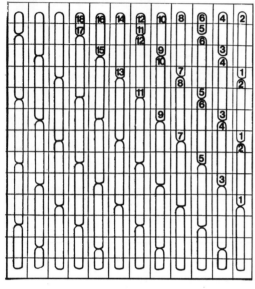

Below: Upright Gobelin in checkerboard for boxes in center design (photo, right)

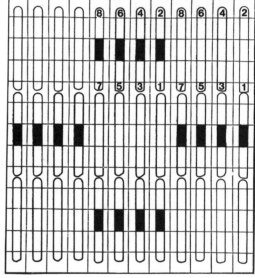

Photo and diagram (below): Upright Gobelin in oval, pattern III, for area (3); for area (4) use pattern horizontally

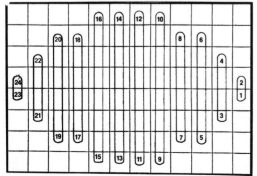

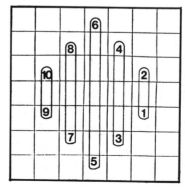

Left: Diamond satin, 2-4-6-4-2 vertical pattern (photo, above)

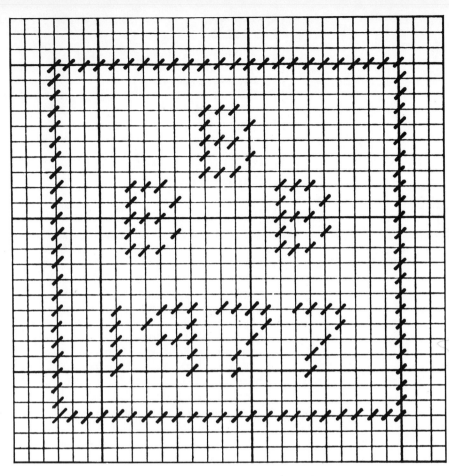

Adding a monogram

Eliminate one of the four baskets in the corners of Nine-Patch, and you can add your monogram and the date you finished your needlepoint. Use continental stitches, both horizontally and vertically, for monogram and background. Work monogram in one color, background in a second color. See section on alphabets and numerals, pages 132–135.

Above: Continental, horizontal (photo, left)

Right: Continental, vertical (photo, below)

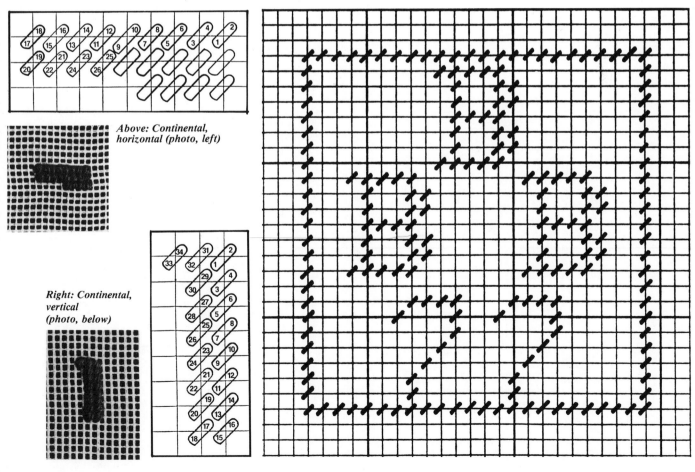

Split Bars

In color, see page 40.

Two versions of the same popular quilt, both bold and colorful and both quietly elegant.

Work needlepoint on a piece of 22½" x 23½" #13 mono interlocked canvas. Approximate size of finished needlepoint is 16½" x 17½". To work wall hanging version, use #7 interlocking needlepoint and rug canvas and pearl cotton #1; see overleaf for instructions.

Circled numbers indicate order in which to work areas of canvas. Letters indicate stitches with which to work areas of canvas. Uncircled numbers indicate colors with which to work areas of canvas.

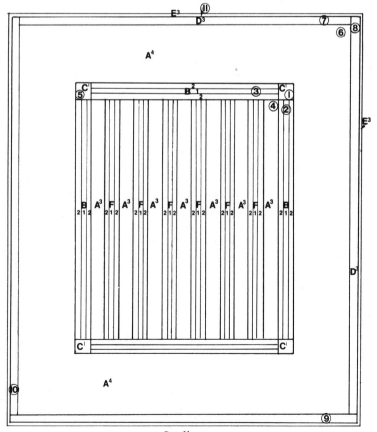

Outline

Stitches

A. upright Gobelin (one-color ripple)
B. Gobelin (zigzag form)
C. rosebud (over 9 mesh)
D. Gobelin, vertical and horizontal patterns
E. continental
F. upright Gobelin (two-color ripple)

Suggested method of working this pattern

Use the complete three-ply strand except for a two-ply continental. Area (1) is begun on right-hand side where arrow directs. There work a rosebud over 9 mesh (opposite below left). Add 10 continental stitches above rosebud in cranberry. (When you later add upright Gobelin stitches to right, the canvas will not show through.) Area (2) is upright Gobelin stitches forming a zigzag (see overleaf left). Work this pattern down right side for 134 mesh. Note: Bottom of this area as well as corresponding stripe on left side ends with a pink stitch over 10 mesh, not 8 mesh as on top. Complete area (2) by working another rosebud as in area (1). Work 10 continental below rosebud. Work Gobelin horizontally forming zigzag across top for 116 mesh for area (3). Work upright Gobelin forming a ripple shape (see overleaf left) for area (4). There are 13 stripes of upright Gobelin (one- and two-color ripples); all stripes are 9 stitches wide. Follow outline for colors. Area (5) repeats area (1): a row of continental above a rosebud. Repeat area (2) down corresponding left side and end side with another rosebud and row of continental. Begin area (6) by working upright Gobelin forming ripple down right side. There will be a total of 74 complete patterns plus one pattern that is worked over only 2 mesh at the bottom. Work area (6) across top. Here there will be a total of 23 complete patterns. Work left side to match right side. Bottom will match top except it is 35 mesh deep instead of 36 as at top. Work area (7) across top using upright Gobelin over 3 mesh. For area (8) work Gobelin horizontally over 3 mesh. Work area (9) on bottom with upright Gobelin (3 mesh). Area (10) matches area (8). Area (11) is two rows of continental on all sides.

Colors	Craft Persian yarn color #	# of 32" strands used
1. med. slate blue	134	59
2. rose pink	130	55
3. forest green	74	104
4. cranberry	9	115

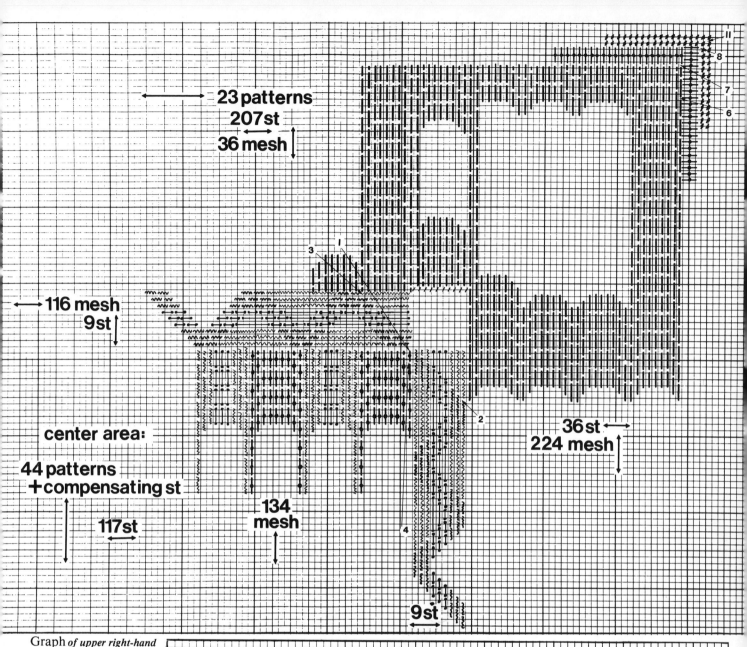

23 patterns
207st
36 mesh

II
8
7
6

3 1

116 mesh
9st

36 st
224 mesh

center area:

44 patterns
+compensating st

117st

134
mesh

2

4

9st

9 st

Graph *of upper right-hand portion*

3	8	16	24	32	33	25	17	9	2
11									6
19									14
27									22
35									30
34									31
26									23
18									15
10									7
1	5	13	21	29	36	28	20	12	4

lower left

upper left

corners:

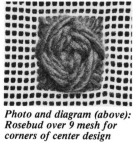

Photo and diagram (above): Rosebud over 9 mesh for corners of center design

Above: Graphs for corners of center pattern

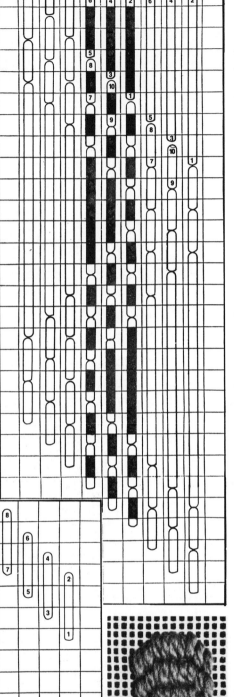

Use these stitches for the center design of the Split Bars needlework on the preceding pages: Gobelin in zigzag design (right and above) for border; upright Gobelin one-color ripple (below and below right) and upright Gobelin two-color ripple (bottom and bottom right) for stripes.

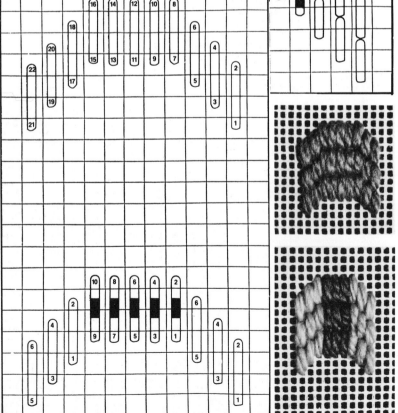

Special Projects

The following eight projects use a variety of canvases and yarns. Six are adaptations of other Amish quilt designs in the book; two are new. There are also instructions for converting different stitches to the continental.

#1 Split Bars

In color, see page 40.

Work wall hanging on a piece of 35″ x 40½″ #7 interlocking needlepoint and rug canvas. Approximate size of finished hanging is 29″ x 34½″.

Stitches

basketweave

Suggested method of working this pattern

Because this canvas is not as rigid as others, it is a good idea to use the basketweave to reduce canvas distortion. Blocking will probably be necessary. When working with pearl cotton #1, start and end a stitch by catching or working over yarn with the next stitch. This yarn is too thick to run it through the back. Follow instructions for working Split Bars on previous pages but use only the basketweave stitch.

D.M.C. pearl cotton #1 color #	# of skeins used
1. 798	8
2. 776	10
3. 3345	13
4. 309	33

Converting to Continental

You may wish to convert some of the stitches shown in this book to the continental or basketweave. To demonstrate how you do this, here is the diamond satin, 2-4-6-4-2 pattern, which was used in the Streak of Lightning needlepoint (right), and a continental version (below right). Each stitch in the diamond satin covers 2, 4, or 6 mesh (except compensating stitches), and each is worked vertically in the spaces between the mesh. Each continental stitch, however, covers 1 mesh on the diagonal. To make the conversion, count how many mesh each diamond satin covers and for that number you must have an equal number of continental stitches. For example, a diamond satin over 2 mesh equals 2 continentals. You may work the continental stitches vertically (below) or horizontally (bottom) to cover the required number of mesh.

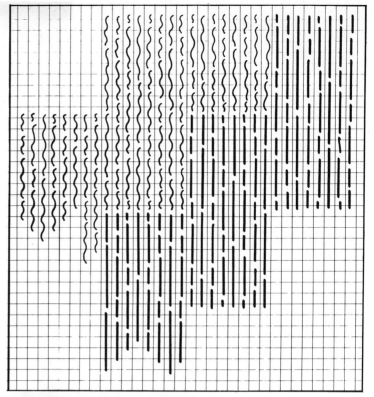

Above:
Diamond satin, 2-4-6-4-2
vertical pattern,
for Streak of
Lightning needlepoint
(photo, left)

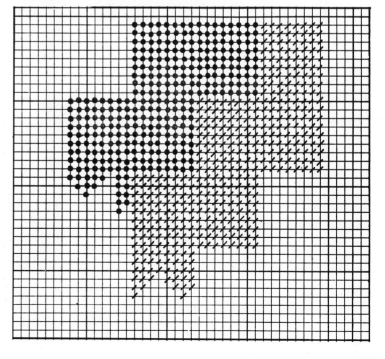

Below:
Continental stitches
for Streak of
Lightning needlepoint

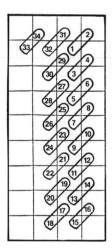

Left:
Continental, vertical
(photo, above)

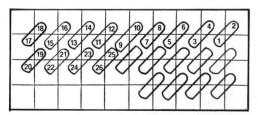

Above:
Continental, horizontal
(photo, right)

Canvases and Yarns

for the eight special projects (pages 82–91)

The designs in this book can all be worked on different-size canvases and with different types of yarns and threads. Here we show the different canvases with yarns that we used for our eight projects. You can also make your own adaptations. Very long stitches (stitches covering many mesh) are not appropriate for rugs in heavily trafficked areas; they can snag easily.

#7 interlocking needlepoint and rug canvas. This interlocking canvas has a heavier weight than mono and is excellent for large wall hangings, for floor pillows, and, if worked in the basketweave stitch, for area rugs. (The continental can be used, but it will distort the canvas more.) With this canvas we used Craft Yarn's Craftacryl rug yarn to produce Rainbow as a wall hanging. The finished design was stretched on heavy-duty mounting board. It could also be hung as a soft tapestry by using a heading at top and at bottom with wooden dowels for support.

#7 interlocking needlepoint and rug canvas. We used this canvas with D.M.C. pearl cotton #1 and the basketweave stitch to make another wall hanging, Split Bars.

#6 rug canvas. This canvas has the same texture as #7. We used it with a thick rug yarn—Paternayan's Pat rug yarn—and bargello stitches to create the hanging or rug, Stars and Stripes. When continental was indicated, we switched to Pat shag rug yarn, which is not as heavy.

#16 mono canvas. Using this canvas, different stitches, and Veloura velvet yarn, we made two interesting pictures or pillows: Four-Patch and Railroad Crossing. You can work the Veloura entirely in basketweave, but then you must use #12 canvas.

#24 cream-colored mono canvas. For our one petit point project—Sunshine and Shadow—we used #24 canvas with D.M.C. embroidery thread and continental or basketweave stitches. Buy the cream-colored canvas rather than the white; it is much finer. You will use just two strands of the six-strand embroidery thread.

#3½ rug canvas. With this canvas and Brunswick Yarn precut wool rug yarn packs, you can latch-hook a rug. Sometimes the #3½ actually has only 3 mesh to the inch. This will vary the finished size, but not the look.

#12 mono interlocked canvas. Combining D.M.C. pearl cotton #3 and continental or basketweave stitches with this canvas, you can make the Baskets quilt as a picture or pillow. Note: A new product, #4 leno canvas, made of 100 percent polyester, comes in both 37- and 61-inch widths. Washable, it is good for a latch-hooked rug. Use with acrylic rug yarn.

#7 interlocking needlepoint and rug canvas with Craftacryl rug yarn

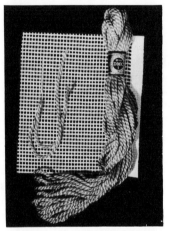

#7 interlocking needlepoint and rug canvas with D.M.C. pearl cotton #1

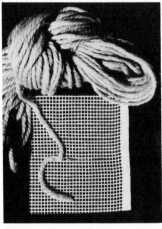

#6 rug canvas with Paternayan's Pat rug yarn

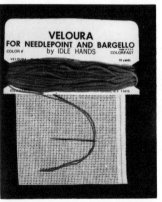

#16 mono canvas with Veloura velvet yarn

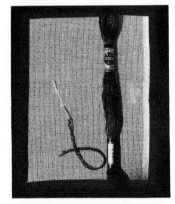

#24 cream-colored mono canvas with D.M.C. embroidery thread

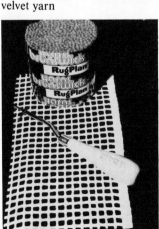

#3½ rug canvas with Brunswick Yarn precut wool rug yarn packs

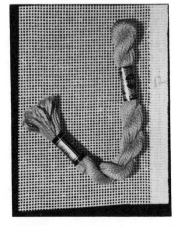

#12 mono interlocked canvas with D.M.C. pearl cotton #3

#2 Sunshine and Shadow

In color, see page 40.

Work doll-size rug on a piece of 12″ x 12″ #24 mono canvas. Approximate size of finished rug is 4¾″ x 4¾″.

Stitches

continental or basketweave

Suggested method of working this pattern

Work this needlepoint with a #22 tapestry needle and two of the six strands of embroidery thread. If #24 canvas is too fine for you, try #18. Use the same graph, but experiment to find the number of strands of thread you need to cover the canvas. With these very fine mesh you must use a hoop. Or work the design on #12 canvas with pearl cotton #3. To work rug, use graph (right top) and outline/color chart (right), which illustrate one quarter section of pattern. Duplicate it in other quarters, turning page 90° for each quarter, so the four outside corners are dark blue.

D.M.C. embroidery thread color #		# of skeins used
1.	310	1
2.	311	1
3.	334	1
4.	775	1
5.	718	1
6.	915	1
7.	902	1
8.	3345	1
9.	909	1
10.	954	1
11.	605	1
12.	209	1
13.	208	1
14.	807	1
15.	796	1

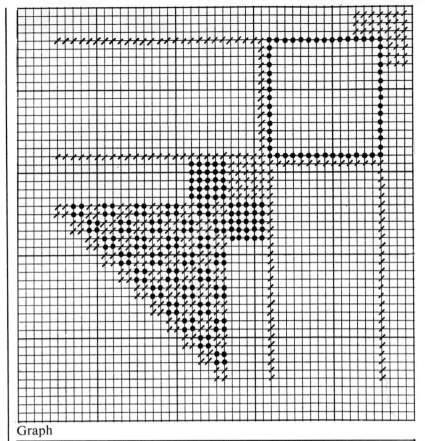

Graph

Outline/Color Chart

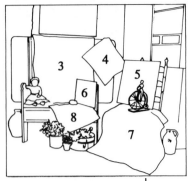

Special projects. #3,
Stars and Stripes;
#4, Railroad
Crossing; #5,
Rainbow; #6, Baskets
or Cake Stand;
#7, Checkerboard;
#8, Four-Patch.
All in color,
see pages 40–41.

#3
Stars and Stripes

Work needlepoint on a piece of
35½″ x 43½″ #6 rug canvas.
Approximate size of finished hanging or
rug is 29½″ x 37½″.

Stitches

diamond satin, 2-4-6-4-2 vertical pattern;
leaf; Gobelin; continental or basketweave

Suggested method of working this pattern

Follow outline, graph, and stitches for the
Stars and Stripes needlepoint on pages
116–119, but work this wall hanging or rug
in Paternayan rug yarn instead of Persian
yarn. Note: Celadon shag is used for
continental or basketweave; rug wool is too
thick for those stitches.

Paternayan's Pat rug yarn color #		# of 32″ strands used
1.	253	120
2.	542	130
3.	305	485

Note: You will also use 75 32″ strands of
celadon shag, #542.

#4
Railroad Crossing

Work needlepoint on 21″ x 21¼″ #16
mono canvas. Approximate size of finished
needlepoint is 15″ x 15¼″.

Stitches

Gobelin; upright Gobelin in diagonal
progression; diagonal rosebud; diagonal
Gobelin; continental or basketweave

Suggested method of working this pattern

Follow instructions for Railroad Crossing
in Persian yarn on pages 102–107, but
substitute velvet yarn for the Persian yarn
and use #16 mono canvas. Work the velvet
yarn with a short strand, preferably 14
inches long, always keeping a short tail. Do
not slide the needle along the yarn or you
will expose its white core. Keep a loose
tension to prevent the canvas from
showing. Work the two-row border in
Persian yarn because the velvet is too thick
to work with continental on #16 canvas.
You can work the velvet yarn all in
continental or basketweave if you use #12
mono interlocked canvas.

	Veloura velvet yarn color #	Amount of Veloura in yards
1.	406	20
2.	403	10
3.	414	10
4.	408	10
5.	429	70
6.	422	20
7.	424	10
8.	402	140
9.	401	20
10.	423	20
11.	405	20
12.	404	10
13.	416	10

#5
Rainbow

Work hanging on a 27″ x 28¾″ #7
interlocking needlepoint and rug canvas.
Approximate size of finished piece is
21″ x 22¾″.

Stitches

basketweave or continental

Suggested method of working this pattern

Because this canvas softens quickly and will require blocking, it is better to use basketweave than continental. Follow graph and outline of Rainbow needlepoint worked with Persian yarn on pages 58–59. Substitute basketweave (or continental) for all stitches. For instructions on how to do so, consult page 83. The finished design is ideal as a hanging, mounted on plywood or Masonite, or, for a soft tapestry, with a casing on top and bottom and a wooden dowel inserted into each casing.

Craftacryl rug yarn color #	# of skeins used
1. 141	1
2. 136	1
3. 134	1
4. 130	1
5. 118	1
6 112	1
7. 148	1
8. 152	3

#6 Baskets

Work needlepoint on a piece of 20″ x 19¼″ #12 mono interlocked canvas. Approximate size of finished piece is 14″ x 13¼″.

Stitches

continental or basketweave

Suggested method of working this pattern

This needlepoint resembles the Baskets needlepoint on pages 122–123, and you follow the outline of that design for placement of turquoise, pink, and green colors. Here, however, there are three differences: this design uses only continental or basketweave (see graph, right); it is worked with pearl cotton #3; there is an extra basket in each row and an extra row (see outline/color chart, above right) for a total of 25 baskets.

D.M.C. pearl cotton #3 color #	# of skeins used
1. 807	8
2. 605	6
3. 904	12

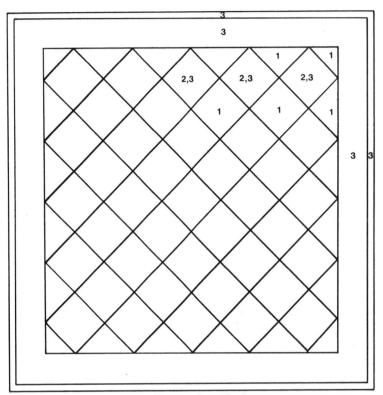

Outline/Color Chart

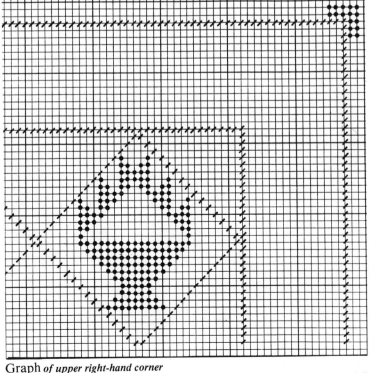

Graph *of upper right-hand corner*

#7 Checkerboard

In color, see pages 40–41.

Work latch-hooked rug on a piece of 37½″ x 45″ #3½ rug canvas. Approximate size of finished rug is 31½″ x 39″.

Stitches

latch-hook

Suggested method of working this pattern

This rug is an adaptation of the Persian yarn Checkerboard needlepoint (pages 70–73). The geometric design and colors can be duplicated in latch-hooking; only the textures must be eliminated. Following the outline of the Persian yarn design and this section graph with color numbers (right top), latch the rug with precut wool rug yarn. Special note: The mesh of this canvas varies slightly from #3½ to #3. The amount of yarn we give is sufficient for either size rug. Brunswick also offers 3.7-mesh polyester rug canvas and acrylic rug yarn which are washable.

Brunswick precut wool rug yarn color #	# of precut packs (320 pieces per pack)
1. 41	14
2. 73	15
3. 31	8
4. 26	8

Basics of latch-hooking

Place canvas on a table with narrow end facing you. Fold about eight rows of end of canvas upward, forming a double layer of canvas at the edge nearest you. Working from left to right through both layers, knot one piece of wool into the first double thread of canvas, skipping the single thread of folding line. Knot the wool only onto those threads that run from selvage to selvage. Work from selvage to selvage, completing each row before starting next. When working, it is helpful to place a weight in middle of rug. To finish: Fold canvas up when about sixteen rows remain to form another double-layered edge. Work the last few rows through double canvas as at the start. Bind the selvages. To make the pile even, trim any long ends.

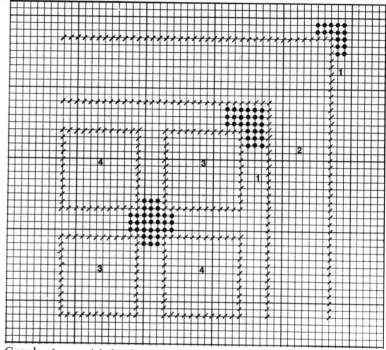

Graph *of upper right-hand corner*   Color Chart

Four easy steps to latch-hook a rug

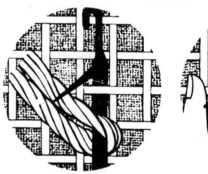

1. Fold a piece of cut wool around latch hook. Fold wool exactly in half; otherwise the pile will be uneven. Push latch hook down through one hole, up through the one immediately in front.

2. Open the latch with your forefinger and place the two ends of the wool into the eye of the hook.

3. Holding the two ends firmly, withdraw the hook back through the loop made by the wool, giving it a twist upward as you do so.

4. Give the two ends of the tuft a slight pull to tighten the knot.

#8 Four-Patch

In color, see pages 40–41.

Work needlepoint on a piece of 15¼″ x 16½″ #16 mono interlocked canvas. Approximate size of finished needlepoint is 9¼″ x 10½″.

Stitches

A. Gobelin, vertical and horizontal patterns
B. small brick, pattern I
C. large brick, pattern II
D. rosebud (over 7 mesh)
E. small brick, pattern I
F. small brick, pattern II
G. two-way Scotch (for diamonds)
  a. solid blue
  b. black and red
  c. black and beige
H. continental or basketweave

Suggested method of working this pattern

Start at area (1), the upper right-hand corner (see graph, next page). Work this box with the small brick, pattern I. In area (2) use large brick, pattern II (see stitch diagram, overleaf left); work to a depth of 3 inches only. Work area (3) with same stitch until 3 inches wide. Now you can begin area (4), which is a rosebud over 7 mesh (see diagram, overleaf right) with a row of continental stitches on all four sides. In area (5) use small brick, pattern I, down the side for 4 inches. Then work this stitch in pattern II across the top in area (6), again for only 4 inches. Begin the center design, which consists of diamonds in different color combinations, but all in a variation of the two-way Scotch stitch (see diagrams, overleaf right). Note different color combinations on outline: **a** is solid blue; **b** is black and red; **c** is black and beige. Complete area (7). Return to area (6) and complete. Then complete area (5). Repeat area (4) at left side of area (6). Work left edge of center design to match area (5). Work a rosebud at each end of bottom of center design. Repeat area (6) below center design between rosebuds. Finish area (2) and area (3), and then work upper left and lower right corner boxes to correspond to area (1). Repeat area (2) on left side of needlepoint and repeat area (3) along bottom. Fill in lower left with a box worked like area (1). Work top and bottom of area (8) in the upright Gobelin stitch over 3 mesh (see diagram, overleaf left). At sides, work stitch in horizontal direction. Note that horizontal Gobelin stitches extend from top to bottom corners, with vertical Gobelin stitches worked between them across top and bottom. To complete needlepoint, work two rows of continental or basketweave on all four sides, area (9).

Special note on working with Veloura: Thread needle with a 14-inch strand, always keeping a short tail of 1 inch. Do not slide the needle on Veloura or its white core will become exposed. Keep a loose tension when stitching to prevent the canvas from showing. Do not run this thread through any stitches on the back; it is too bulky. Work stitches over the tails. If you want to use only the basketweave, use a #12 mono interlocked canvas. Your finished work on #12 canvas will be about 12½″ x 14″.

Veloura velvet yarn color #	# of yards used
1. 402	60
2. 404	70
3. 432	80
4. 423	40
5. 417	10

Circled numbers indicate order in which to work areas of canvas.
Letters indicate stitches with which to work areas of canvas.
Uncircled numbers indicate colors with which to work areas of canvas.

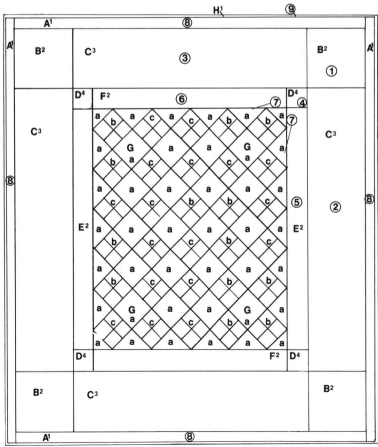

Outline

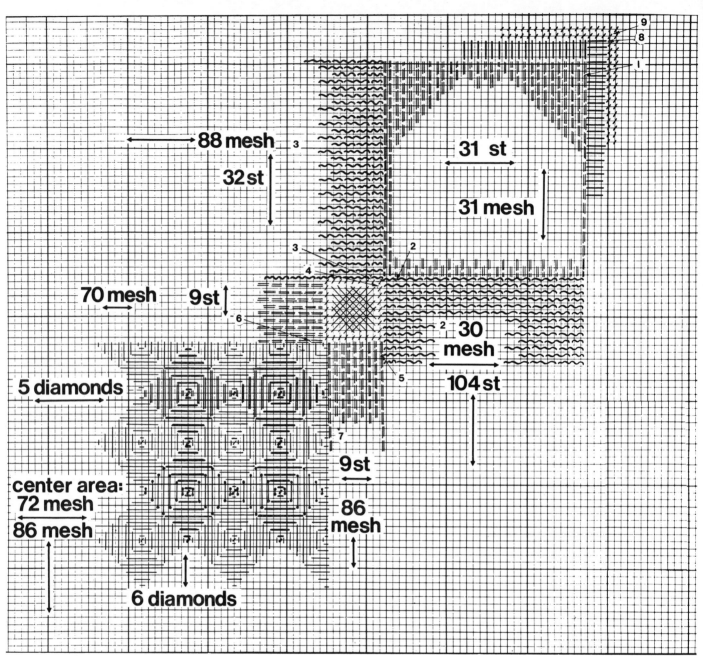

88 mesh 3

32 st

31 st

31 mesh

70 mesh **9 st**

3

4

2

30 mesh

6

5 diamonds

2

104 st

5

7

center area: 72 mesh

9 st

86 mesh

86 mesh

6 diamonds

9
8
I

Graph *of upper right-hand portion of Four-Patch*

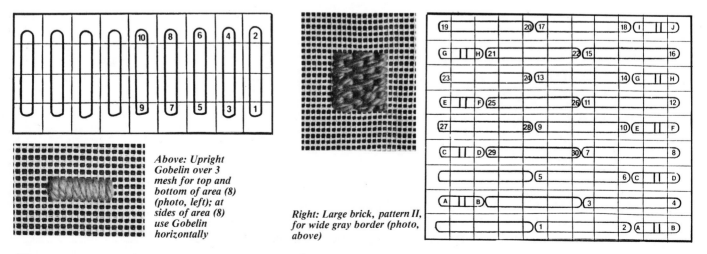

Above: Upright Gobelin over 3 mesh for top and bottom of area (8) (photo, left); at sides of area (8) use Gobelin horizontally

Right: Large brick, pattern II, for wide gray border (photo, above)

3	8	16	24	25	17	9	2
11							6
19							14
27							22
26							23
18							15
10							7
1	5	13	21	28	20	12	4

Left: Rosebud over 7 mesh for small corners (photo, below)

Photo and diagram (below): Two-way Scotch stitches forming diamonds in three color combinations for the center design of needlepoint

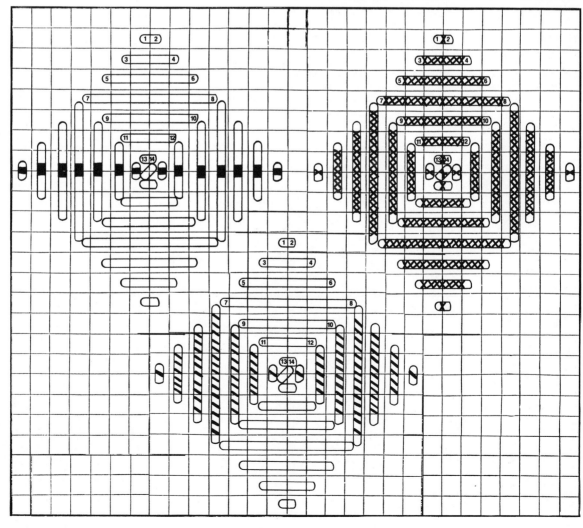

Improved Nine-Patch

In color, see page 42.

Only three colors and all deep tones—plum, red, blue—give this needlework its very intense quality.

Work needlepoint on a piece of 21½″ x 22½″ #12 mono interlocked canvas. Approximate size of finished needlepoint is 15½″ x 16½″.

Circled numbers indicate order in which to work areas of canvas.
Letters indicate stitches with which to work areas of canvas.
Uncircled numbers indicate colors with which to work areas of canvas.

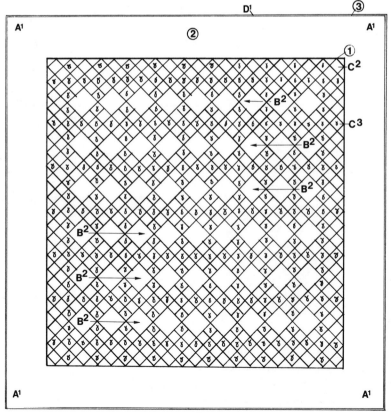

Outline

Stitches

A. large brick, pattern I
B. diagonal rosebud (over 16 mesh)
C. diamond satin, 2-4-6-8-6-4-2 horizontal pattern
D. continental or basketweave

Suggested method of working this pattern

For all stitches use the complete three-ply strand, except for the continental or basketweave which requires two plies. Start at area (1). Work a diamond satin, 2-4-6-8-6-4-2 horizontal pattern (opposite below left), in red. Work pattern across top row following colors on outline, red when there is a blank diamond and blue when the diamond has a squiggle mark. Work row after row in this manner (opposite below right). The larger diamonds marked B^2, however, are diagonal rosebuds over 16 mesh (below), worked in red. Complete center design, following outline and graph. Work area (2) with large brick, pattern I. Start in upper right-hand corner: work down right side, across top, down left side, across bottom. Area (3) is two rows of continental or basketweave on all sides.

Colors	Craft Persian yarn color #	# of 32″ strands used
1. plum	125	85
2. rhubarb	16	132
3. blueberry	86	65

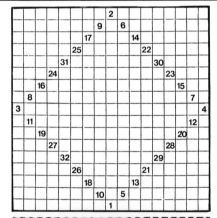

Photo and diagram: Diagonal rosebud over 16 mesh for large diamonds in center design

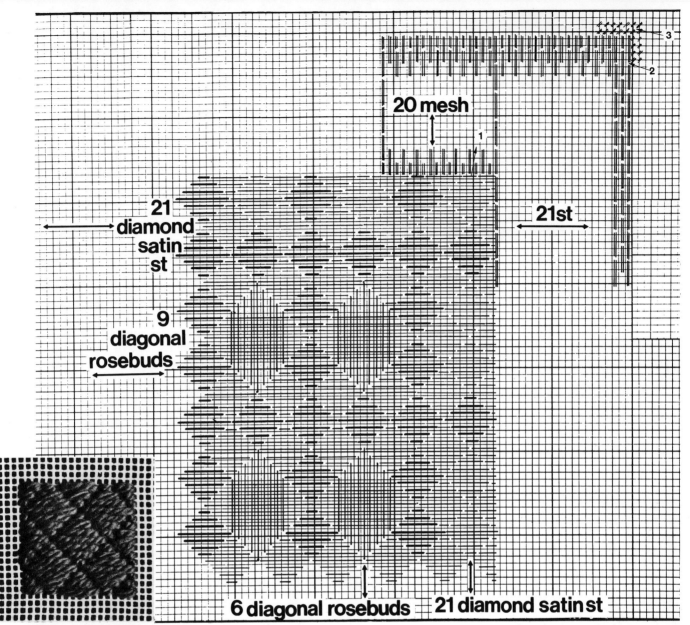

20 mesh

3

2

1

21 diamond satin st

21st

9 diagonal rosebuds

6 diagonal rosebuds — 21 diamond satin st

Below: Diamond satin, 2-4-6-8-6-4-2 horizontal pattern, for small diamonds in center design (photo, above)

Graph *of upper right-hand portion*

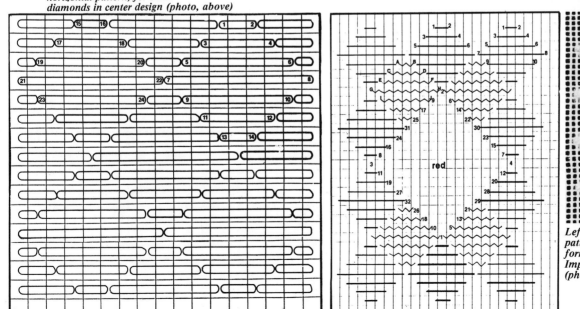

red

Left: Diamond satin patterns in two colors to form center design of Improved Nine-Patch (photo, above)

Variable Star

In color, see page 42.

Stitches

A. Gobelin, vertical and horizontal patterns
B. diamond satin, 2-4-6-8-6-4-2 vertical pattern
C. Gobelin (for stars)
D. continental

Suggested method of working this pattern

For all stitches use the complete three-ply strand except for the continental which requires two plies. In area (1) begin the plum background in the diamond satin, 2-4-6-8-6-4-2 vertical pattern. Work it across the top from the right to the left side. There will be a total of 26 complete diamond satin patterns across in plum. Next work the variable stars (opposite below) on the top row of center design area (2a). You must consult the six special color variation diagrams near the outline. There will be a total of 5 multicolored stars in each row. Next fill in the plum background between the stars in the first row, area (2b). Then work the plum background in diamond satin down the right side, 34 patterns deep, area (3). Work a row of stars across area (4a), consulting the special diagrams for color combinations. Then fill in the plum background in area (4b). Continue in this manner until the entire center is worked. Next work the diamond satins in 2-4-6-8-6-4-2 vertical pattern in area (10), across the bottom and along the left side. Like the top background, the bottom will be 26 diamond satin patterns wide; like the right side, the left side will be 34 patterns deep. Work upright Gobelin over 4 mesh across top and bottom from right to left, area (11). Then work the Gobelin horizontally along the sides, area (12). Area (13) consists of two rows of continental around the entire design.

Stars in different color combinations float in a deep plum sea, framed by a narrow blue border.

Work the needlepoint on a piece of 22″ x 26″ #12 mono interlocked canvas. Approximate size of finished needlepoint is 16″ x 20″.

Circled numbers indicate order in which to work areas of canvas.
Letters indicate stitches with which to work areas of canvas.
Uncircled numbers indicate colors with which to work areas of canvas.
Six special small star diagrams explain color combinations.

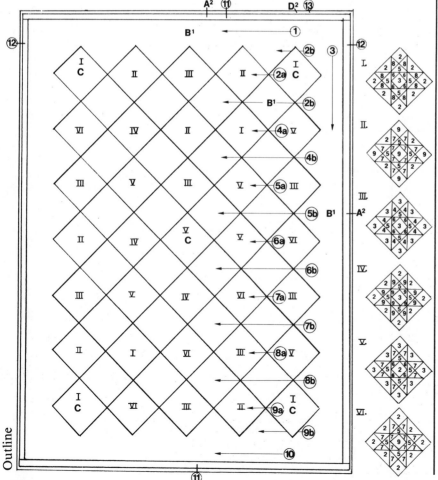

Outline

Colors	Craft Persian yarn color #	# of 32″ strands used
1. deep plum	124	260
2. deep slate blue	132	57
3. storm blue	117	35
4. French blue	116	22
5. black	96	25
6. pewter	98	17
7. burgundy	17	34
8. peach	23	8
9. wheat	104	20

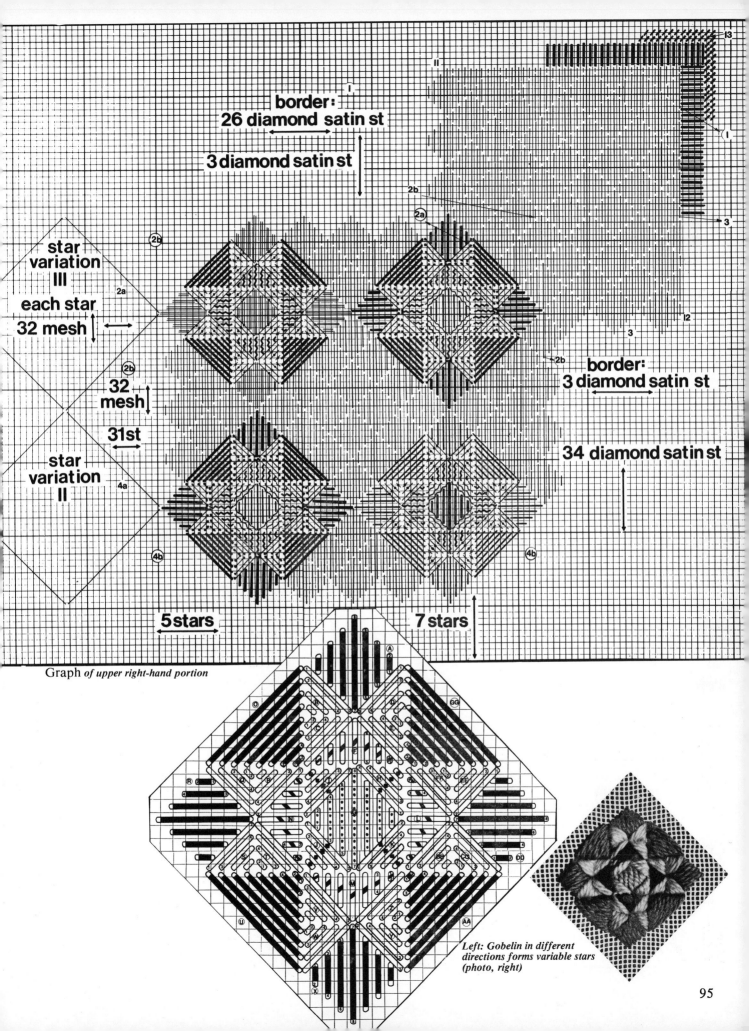

border:
26 diamond satin st

3 diamond satin st

star
variation
III

each star

32 mesh

2b

32
mesh

31st

star
variation
II

2a

2b

4a

4b

2a

2b

2b

3

border:
3 diamond satin st

34 diamond satin st

5 stars

7 stars

Graph *of upper right-hand portion*

*Left: Gobelin in different
directions forms variable stars
(photo, right)*

Diamond
In color, see page 42.

The diamond in its simplest form is an interpretation of the central-medallion quilts of eighteenth-century Europe.

Work the needlepoint on a piece of 20″ x 20½″ #12 mono interlocked canvas. Approximate size of finished needlepoint is 14″ x 14½″.

Circled numbers indicate order in which to work areas of canvas.
Letters indicate stitches with which to work areas of canvas.
Uncircled numbers indicate colors with which to work areas of canvas.

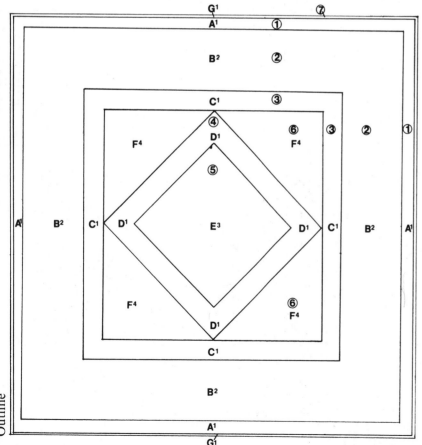

Stitches

A. small brick, pattern I
B. diamond satin, 2-4-6-8-6-4-2 vertical pattern
C. continental or basketweave
D. continental or basketweave
E. Parisian
F. small brick, pattern II
G. continental or basketweave

Suggested method of working this pattern

For all stitches use the complete three-ply strand, except for the continental or basketweave which requires two plies. Begin needlepoint in area (1), top right-hand corner. Work small brick, pattern I, for 4 inches across top and for 4 inches down right side. Area (2) begins near upper right corner. Work diamond satin, 2-4-6-8-6-4-2 vertical pattern (opposite below left), across the top to left. The area should be 21 diamond satins wide. Work the same pattern 21 diamond satins deep down right side. In the same pattern work down the left side, then across the bottom. After you have established this frame, complete area (1) on all sides. In area (3) work continental or basketweave. For area (4) count in 51 unworked mesh from right side and start stitching continental or basketweave in the 52nd space as on graph (opposite top). You will stitch a diamond in this area. It is easiest to execute if you first outline the diamond in sewing thread. Area (5) consists of Parisian stitches (opposite below right). Work area (6), triangular shapes surrounding the diamond, in small brick, pattern II. Work it loosely so that the canvas does not show. After completing these four areas, you may have to add another row of continental around diamond to prevent canvas from showing. Work two rows of continental or basketweave in area (7) on all four sides.

Colors	Craft Persian yarn color #	# of 32″ strands used
1. pale blue	83	71
2. burgundy	17	80
3. poppy red	18	20
4. leaf green	56	42

Outline

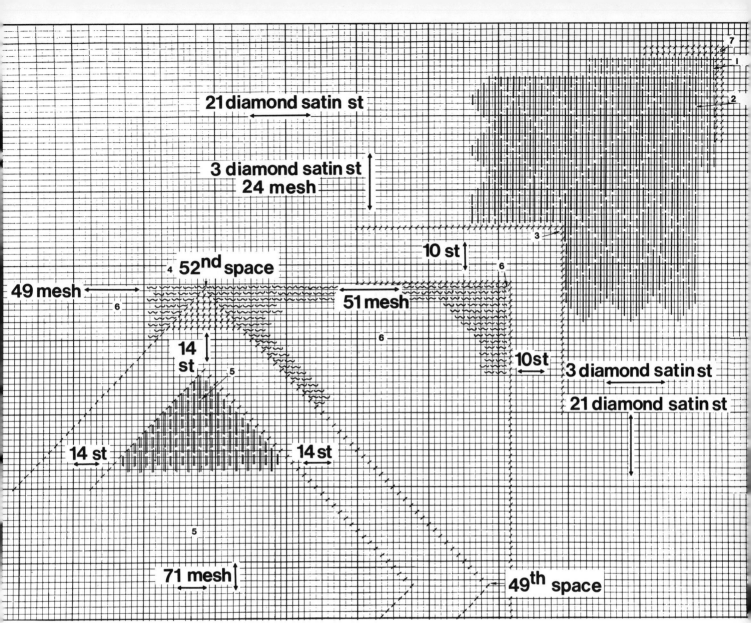

21 diamond satin st

**3 diamond satin st
24 mesh**

49 mesh

4 **52nd space**

6

10 st

6

51 mesh

6

**14
st**

5

14 st

14 st

10 st

3 diamond satin st

21 diamond satin st

5

71 mesh

49th space

7

1

2

3

6

Graph *of upper right quarter*

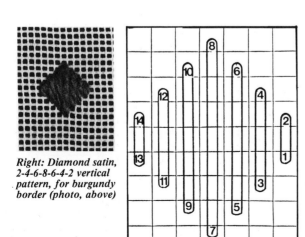

Right: *Diamond satin,
2-4-6-8-6-4-2 vertical
pattern, for burgundy
border (photo, above)*

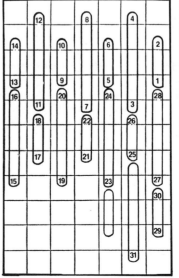

Left: *Parisian stitches
for center of diamond
(photo, above)*

Lone Star

In color, see page 43.

For a glowing star in a multitude of colors, even the quilt's scalloped border has been duplicated in needlework.

Work needlepoint on a piece of 22″ x 22½″ #13 mono interlocked canvas. Approximate size of finished needlepoint is 16″ x 16½″.

Circled numbers indicate order in which to work areas of canvas. Letters indicate stitches with which to work areas of canvas. Uncircled numbers indicate colors with which to work areas of canvas. For colors in star, see color chart (overleaf left).

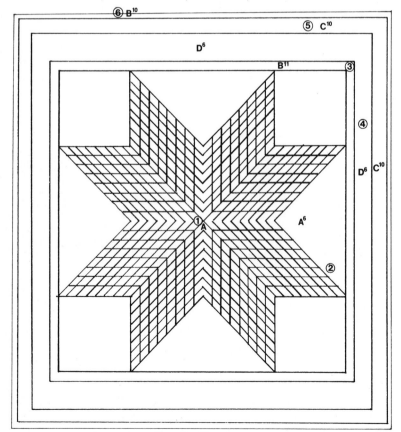

Outline

Stitches

A. Gobelin in diagonal progression, vertical and horizontal patterns
B. continental or basketweave
C. buttonhole
D. upright Gobelin in diagonal progression

Suggested method of working this pattern

For all stitches use the complete three-ply strand, except for the continental or basketweave which requires two plies. Area (1), at the center of the needlepoint, begins the star. Measure down from top edge of canvas 11¼ inches and in from side edge 11 inches. From this point count down and start working star center according to diagram (overleaf right top). Consult color chart and list (overleaf left) and diagram (overleaf right below). You will see that the colors move around the star as the arrows direct. If there is an exception, the different color is underlined on star color chart. Complete the star. Next work area (2), around the star, in Gobelin in diagonal progression over 5 mesh. Be sure to work Gobelin stitches in the directions shown on graph (opposite top). For area (3) use continental or basketweave. For area (4) use upright Gobelin over 5 mesh in diagonal progression. Note: Border on top is 15 mesh deep, at side only 7 stitches wide. Before starting area (5), work one row of vertical continental in navy along right side of area (4) (see graph). Work corresponding area on left side of needlepoint. Then work buttonhole stitch (below) all around design, area (5). Note: Buttonhole at corners has a different count from other buttonhole stitches. Fill in around buttonholes with continental. Area (6) is two more rows of continental.

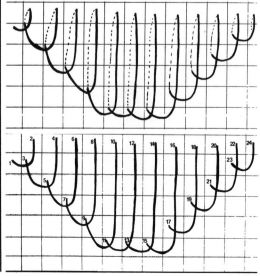

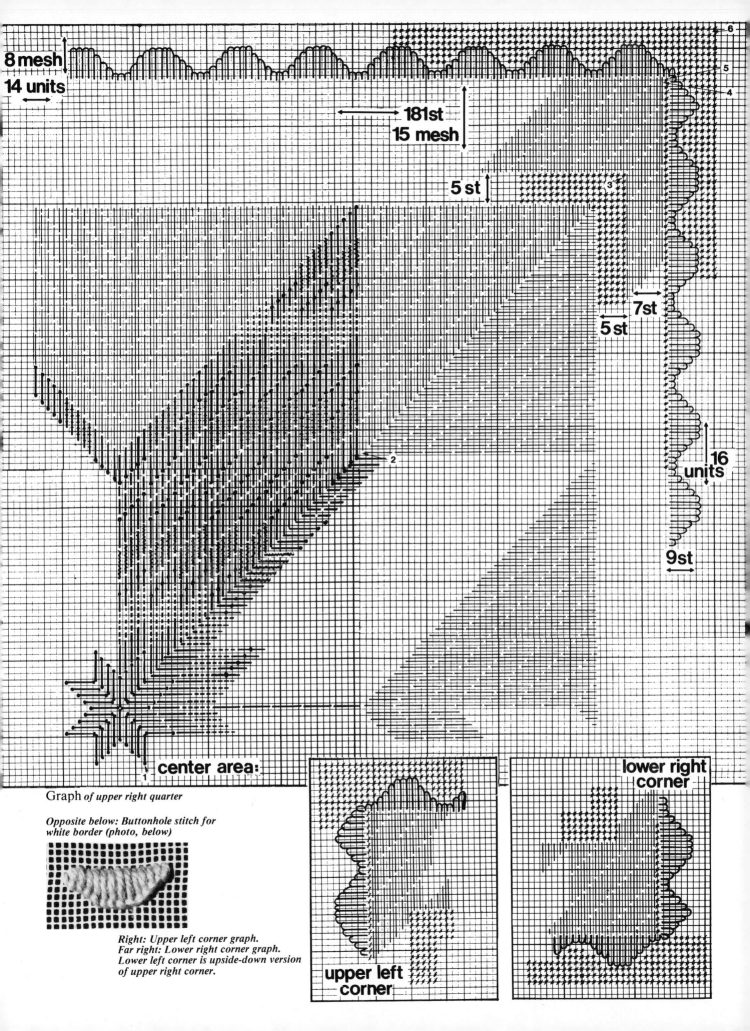

8 mesh

14 units

181st
15 mesh

5 st

5 st

7 st

16 units

9 st

2

1

center area:

Graph *of upper right quarter*

Opposite below: Buttonhole stitch for
white border (photo, below)

Right: Upper left corner graph.
Far right: Lower right corner graph.
Lower left corner is upside-down version
of upper right corner.

upper left
corner

lower right
corner

Colors	Craft Persian yarn color #	# of 32'' strands used
1. peach	23	17
2. creamy orange	32	13
3. maize	44	9
4. lime green	70	12
5. violet blue	89	6
6. navy	95	248
7. black	96	12
8. blue gray	97	25
9. pale gray	100	8
10. white	101	79
11. celadon	114	85
12. pink beige	139	19

Color Chart *for star*

Right: Gobelin over 5 mesh in diagonal progression to form center of star (photo, above)

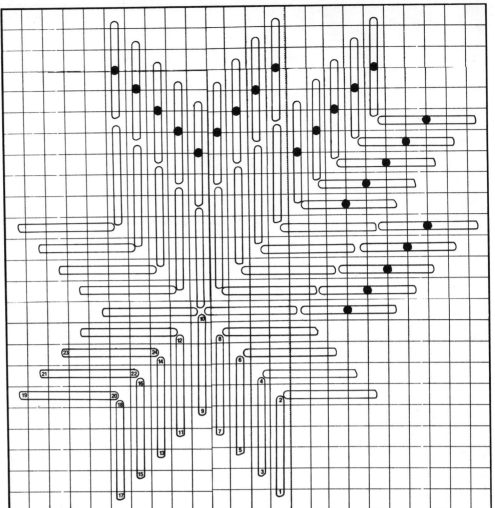

Left: Gobelin over 5 mesh in diagonal progression in different colors to form star (photo, below)

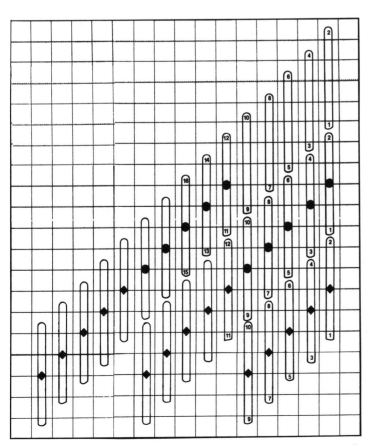

Railroad Crossing

In color, see pages 44–45.

Tiny triangles in an endless array of colors are restrained within bold black X forms and a black border.

Work the needlepoint on a piece of 25″ x 24″ #13 mono interlocked canvas. Approximate size of finished needlepoint is 19″ x 18″.

Circled numbers indicate order in which to work areas of canvas.
Letters indicate stitches with which to work areas of canvas.
Uncircled numbers indicate colors with which to work areas of canvas.
See special color chart, page 106, for colors of tiny triangles.

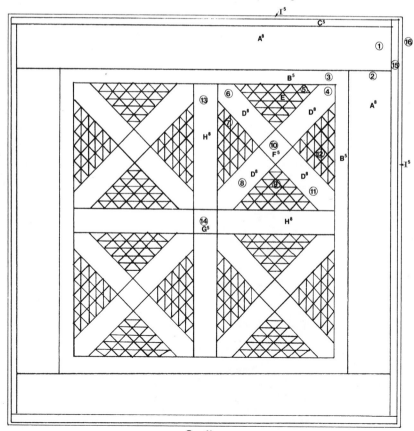

Outline

Stitches

A. Gobelin (border pattern)
B. Gobelin (wave pattern)
C. Gobelin, vertical and horizontal patterns
D. upright Gobelin in diagonal progression
E. Gobelin (for tiny triangles)
F. diagonal rosebud (over 20 mesh)
G. Gobelin (center triangles)
H. diagonal Gobelin
I. continental, horizontal and vertical

Suggested method of working this pattern

For all stitches use the complete three-ply strand except for the continental which requires two plies. The following instructions apply to the upper right-hand box, Box 1, and surrounding areas (see graph, opposite above). The other three boxes (see outline, below left) are worked in similar fashion. The only changes are the colors of the small triangles. That information is given on the special color chart, page 106. Start at area (1), using Gobelin in border pattern. Border pattern consists of stitches in oval, pattern I (see diagram, page 106), surrounded by more Gobelin stitches (page 107). Work across the top until you complete 8 ovals. Add 1 extra stitch over 2 mesh before you start the 9th oval. (There will therefore be 3 stitches of equal height in this one area. All the other ovals have only 2 stitches of equal height next to each other.) Continue across top until there are a total of 16 ovals. Complete this area with rows of Gobelin above and below the ovals (see graph). Work area (2) with the same design as area (1). Work 6 ovals down, add extra stitch before starting 7th oval, and continue until you have a total of 13 complete ovals. Work stitches surrounding ovals. Work area (3) with Gobelin in wave pattern (see overleaf left below). Complete 8 waves, then add extra stitch. Continue until there are a total of 16 waves. Return to where you started, area (3), and copy corner on graph and diagram, page 107. Continue down right side with waves until there are 6 complete patterns. Add extra stitch and continue until there are 13 waves. Fill in around waves and top corner. Start area (4) using upright Gobelin in diagonal progression. Begin the first group of tiny triangles, area (5)(A). (See stitch diagram, overleaf right top, for stitching them, and color chart, page 106, for coloring them.) Work across one row of triangles at a time until you complete this area. Work area (6), small triangles in area (7)(D), area (8), area (9)(C).

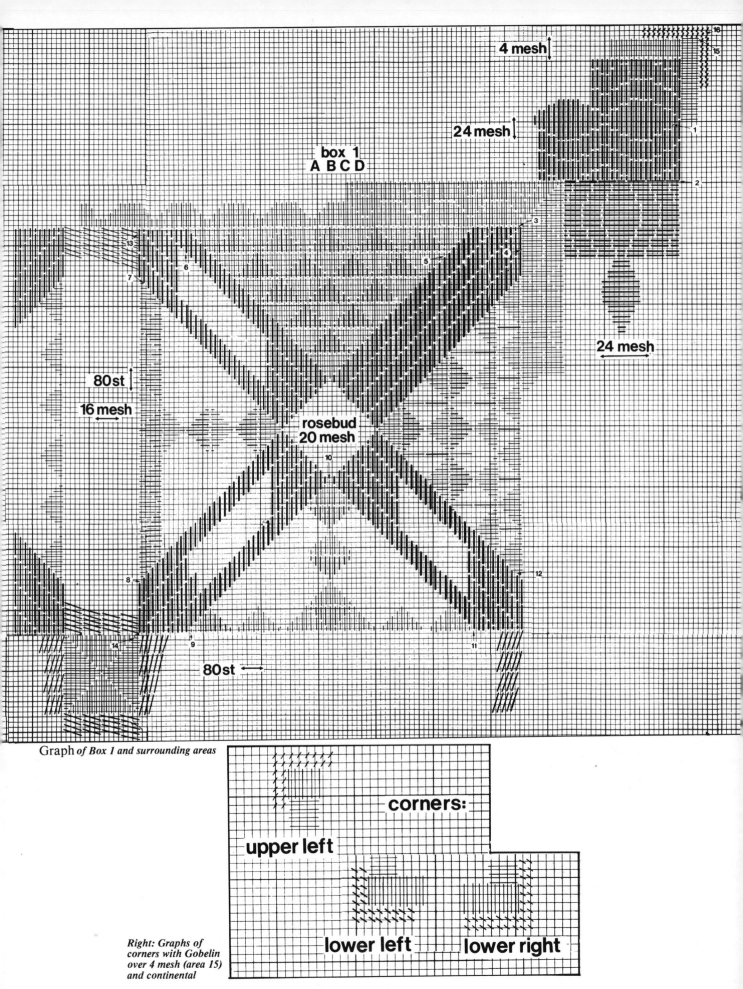

4 mesh

box 1
A B C D

24 mesh

16

15

1

2

3

13

6

4

5

7

24 mesh

80 st

16 mesh

rosebud
20 mesh

10

8

12

14   9   11

80 st →

Graph *of Box 1 and surrounding areas*

corners:

upper left

Right: Graphs of
corners with Gobelin
over 4 mesh (area 15)
and continental

lower left   **lower right**

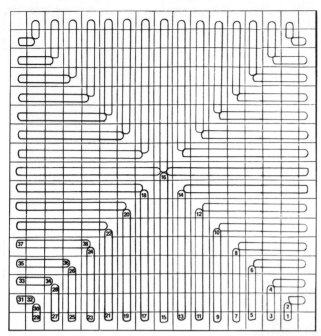

Above: Gobelin for four triangles in center of needlepoint (photo, right)

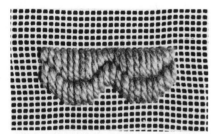

Below: Gobelin in wave pattern for area (3) (photo, left)

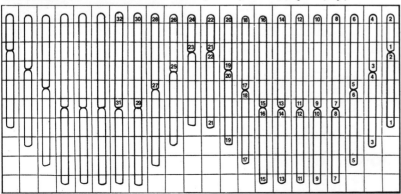

Then work area (10), which is a diagonal rosebud over 20 mesh (opposite left below). Work area (11) and area (12)(B). You have now completed Box 1. Move to area (13) and work the diagonal Gobelin over 4 mesh. Area (14) is the center square composed of 4 large triangles (left top and page 106). Next work Box 3 in same manner as Box 1, but with different colors. Work area (2) down corresponding left side of design. Continue area (3) down left side. Work Box 4, then the three other corresponding areas of area (13). Work Box 2. Complete area (3) across bottom. Work area on bottom corresponding to area (1). Starting in upper right-hand corner, follow graph and outline for area (15): Gobelin over 4 mesh, horizontally at sides and vertically at top and bottom. (See corner graphs, previous page.) Work area (16), two rows of continental on all sides (opposite right below): horizontal on top and bottom and vertical at sides.

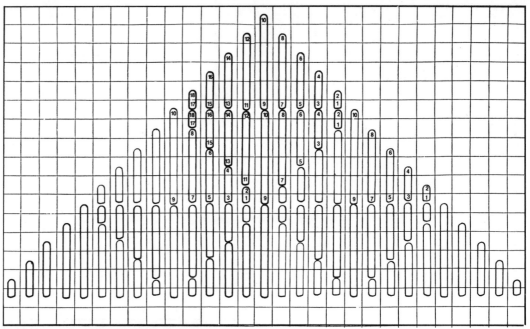

Above: Gobelin for tiny triangles (photo, left)

Below: Diagonal rosebud over 20 mesh (photo, left)

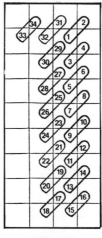

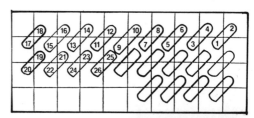

Above: Horizontal continental (photo, right)

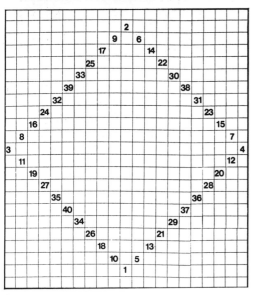

Left above: Vertical continental (photo, left)

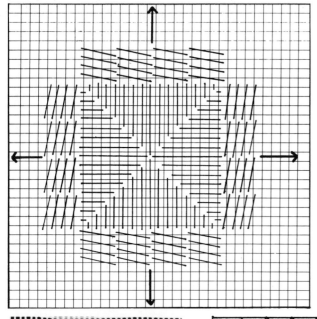

Colors	Craft Persian yarn color #	# of 32'' strands used
1. flesh	22	12
2. rust	37	12
3. antique bronze	54	12
4. army green	55	12
5. pale blue	83	75
6. sea blue	84	20
7. navy	95	12
8. black	96	145
9. white	101	15
10. French blue	116	12
11. rose pink	130	15
12. pale rose	131	12
13. orange rust	356	6

Photo and diagram (above): Gobelin forming four triangles in center of needlepoint surrounded by diagonal Gobelin

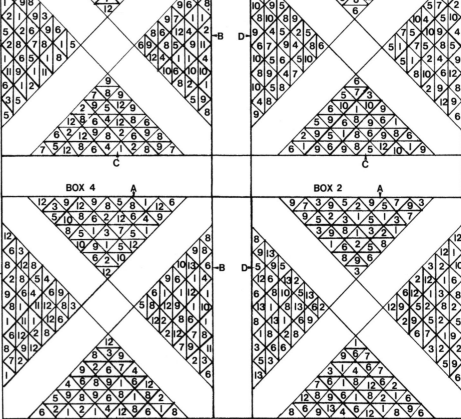

Color Chart *for tiny triangles*

Left: Gobelin in oval, pattern I (photo, left above)

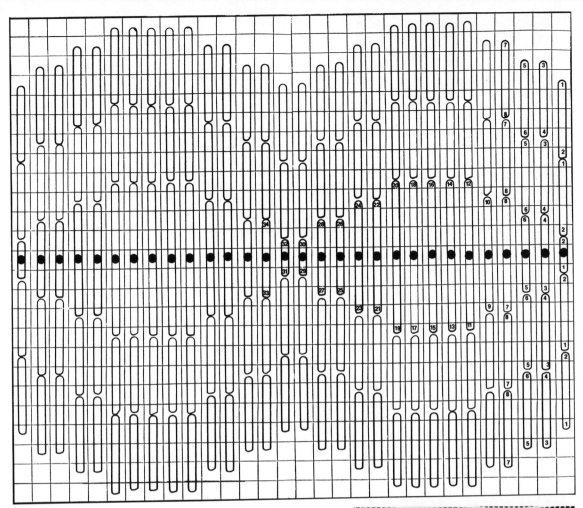

Above: Gobelin in oval, pattern I, surrounded by Gobelin stitches (photo, right); two different colors were used to illustrate this pattern, but use only black when you stitch

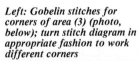

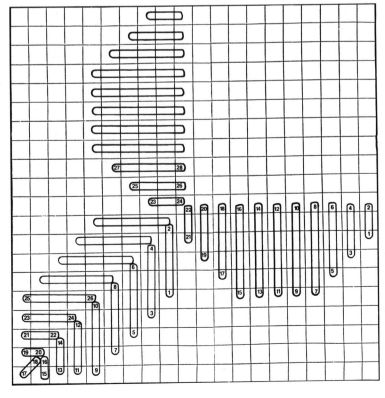

Left: Gobelin stitches for corners of area (3) (photo, below); turn stitch diagram in appropriate fashion to work different corners

Log Cabin-Straight Furrow

In color, see page 45.

Four shades of red and four shades of green form a subtle Log Cabin pattern, a quilt rarely made by the Amish.

Work the needlepoint on a piece of 21″ x 20″ #12 mono interlocked canvas. Approximate size of finished needlepoint is 15″ x 14″.

Circled numbers indicate order in which to work areas of canvas.
Letters indicate stitches with which to work areas of canvas.
Uncircled numbers indicate colors with which to work areas of canvas.

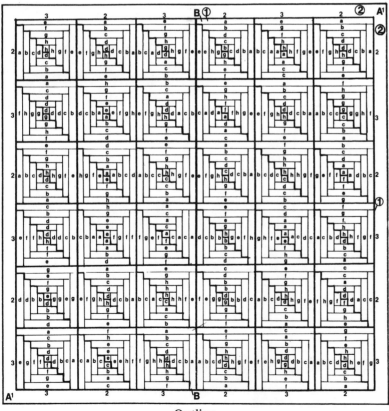

Outline

Stitches

A. continental or basketweave
B. Gobelin, vertical and horizontal patterns

Suggested method of working this pattern

For all stitches use the complete three-ply strand, except for the continental or basketweave which requires two plies. Surrounding the four shades of red and four shades of green in the center design area of this needlepoint is a red border. The reds are subdivided under the number 2 with letters for the different shades (a, b, c, d), and the greens are labeled number 3 plus letters (e, f, g, h). First work area (1), which consists of 36 patterned squares. See opposite page for placement of Gobelin stitches to form each box. Complete the entire top row of squares. Then work other rows. Work area (2), the border, in eight rows of continental or basketweave stitches.

Colors	Craft Persian yarn color #	# of 32″ strands used
1. poppy red	18	36
2a. cranberry	9	31
2b. strawberry	10	38
2c. dusty red	11	33
2d. red rose	12	23
3e. dark olive	112	32
3f. olive	113	34
3g. celadon	114	29
3h. pale mint	115	23

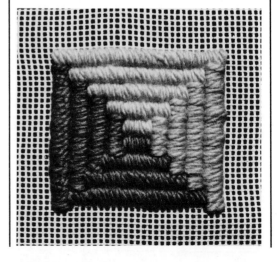

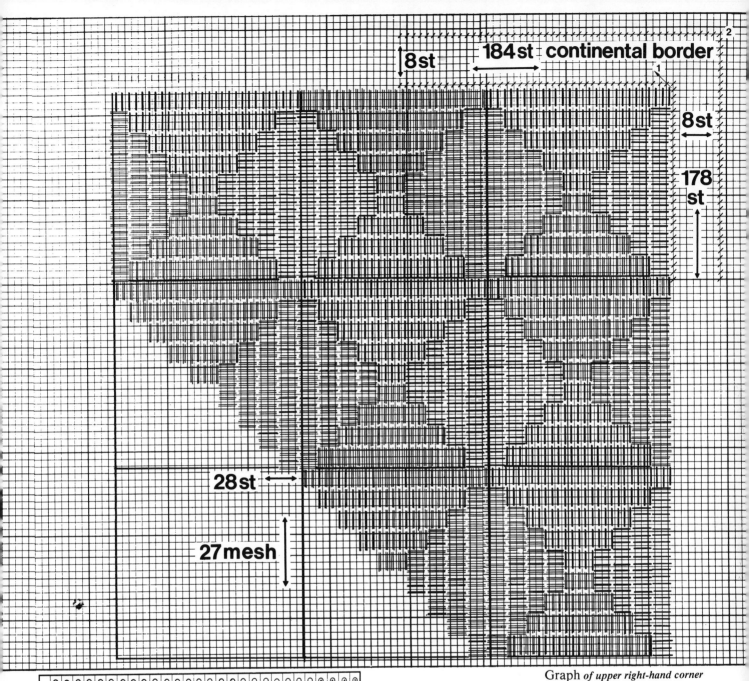

8st

184 st : continental border

8st

178 st

28st

27mesh

Graph *of upper right-hand corner*

Left: Gobelin, vertical and horizontal directions, to form squares for center design area of Log Cabin (photo, opposite below right)

Streak of Lightning

In color, see page 45.

Bold streaks of black and red march across this canvas, framed by a wide olive-green border.

Work needlepoint on a piece of 18½″ x 19½″ #12 mono interlocked canvas. Approximate size of finished needlepoint is 12½″ x 13½″.

Circled numbers indicate order in which to work areas of canvas.
Letters indicate stitches with which to work areas of canvas.
Uncircled numbers indicate colors with which to work areas of canvas.

Outline

Stitches

A. Parisian
B. continental
C. diamond satin, 2-4-6-4-2 vertical pattern
D. continental or basketweave

Suggested method of working this pattern

For all stitches use the complete three-ply strand, except for the continental or basketweave which requires two plies. Area (1) is begun in the upper right-hand corner of the center design, marked C^3 on outline. Using the graph, count in and work the first streak in black. You will use the diamond satin, 2-4-6-4-2 vertical pattern (see stitch diagram, opposite below left). Work the first black streak from upper right corner down to bottom left corner. Fill in the entire center with alternating streaks of black (C^3) and red (C^2). Now work one row of continental across the top of area (1) in olive and across the bottom of area (1) before beginning area (2). Start area (2) in the center of the right border at arrow. Here you will use the Parisian in an elongated diamond. Again, consult graph, outline, and stitch diagram (opposite below right) for forming this design. Work this pattern all along the right side. Work Parisian in elongated diamonds in area (3), across the top, across the bottom, and along left border. You do not have to begin in mid-row as you did when you started area (2). Use the continental to fill in around Parisian. For area (4) work two rows of continental or basketweave around design.

Colors	Craft Persian yarn color #	# of 32″ strands used
1. olive	113	90
2. poppy red	18	65
3. black	96	65

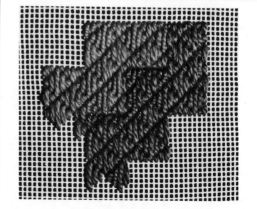

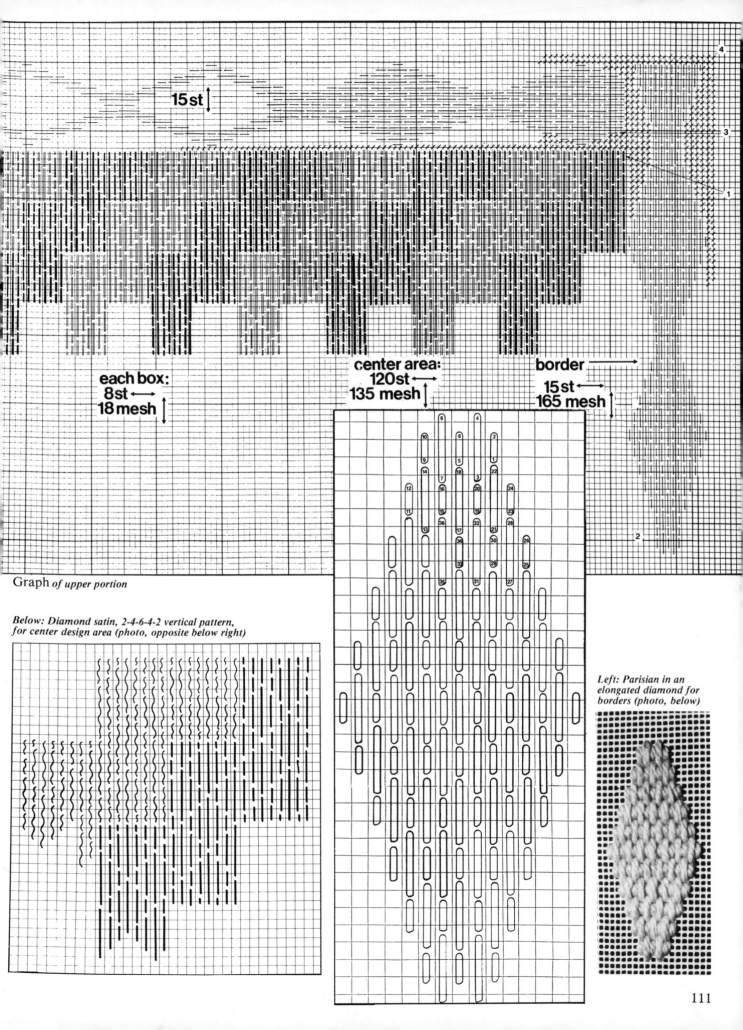

15 st

each box:
8 st ←→
18 mesh ↕

center area:
120 st ←→
135 mesh ↕

border →
15 st ←→
165 mesh ↕

Graph *of upper portion*

Below: *Diamond satin, 2-4-6-4-2 vertical pattern,*
for center design area (photo, opposite below right)

Left: Parisian in an
elongated diamond for
borders (photo, below)

111

Baby's Block Variation

In color, see page 46.

An unusual pattern: blocks worked in rich shades of nutmeg, plum, green tumble down the center.

Work needlepoint on a piece of 19 1/2'' x 21 1/4'' #13 mono interlocked canvas. Approximate size of finished needlepoint is 13 1/2'' x 15 1/4''.

Circled numbers indicate order in which to work areas of canvas.
Letters indicate stitches with which to work areas of canvas.
Uncircled numbers indicate colors with which to work areas of canvas.

Outline

Stitches

A. stem
B. upright Gobelin (chevron design)
C. Gobelin, horizontal pattern (for block)
D. diagonal Gobelin (for block)
E. upright Gobelin (wing pattern)
F. continental or basketweave

Suggested method of working this pattern

For all stitches use the complete three-ply strand, except for the continental or basketweave which requires two plies. Begin the needlepoint in the upper right-hand corner of area (1) using the upright Gobelin in a wing pattern (overleaf left). Work the area 6 patterns wide, filling in with compensating continental stitches as graph directs (opposite top). Work the same pattern down the right side for 4 inches, again including compensating continental stitches. Move to area (2) and fill in with stem stitch as wide as you have worked area (1). Proceed to right side and work stem downward for approximately 4 inches. Now you are ready to begin the first line of baby's blocks, area (3). First work the inside portion, C^2, with Gobelin in a horizontal direction (overleaf). Then work the outside portions with diagonal Gobelin (see overleaf right) in nutmeg on top and green below. Work the entire length of the row according to outline (left). Fill in surrounding areas with continental stitches, F^5. Next move to area (4), which you work in upright Gobelin stitches that form a chevron design (overleaf left). Work row all the way down. Complete the entire center design area: 5 stripes of blocks and 4 stripes of chevron patterns. Complete area (2) on all four sides of center design area. Complete area (1). Note that the 7th pattern on the top and bottom is 2 stitches smaller than all the others; 21st pattern on the sides is worked over fewer mesh.
For area (5) work continental or basketweave on all four sides for five rows. Note how stitches on side slant inward (see special diagram, opposite below). Turn the canvas to work sides easily.

Colors	Craft Persian yarn color #	# of 32'' strands used
1. med. slate blue	134	80
2. light plum	126	52
3. army green	55	49
4. nutmeg	38	49
5. light gold	45	39
6. black	96	23

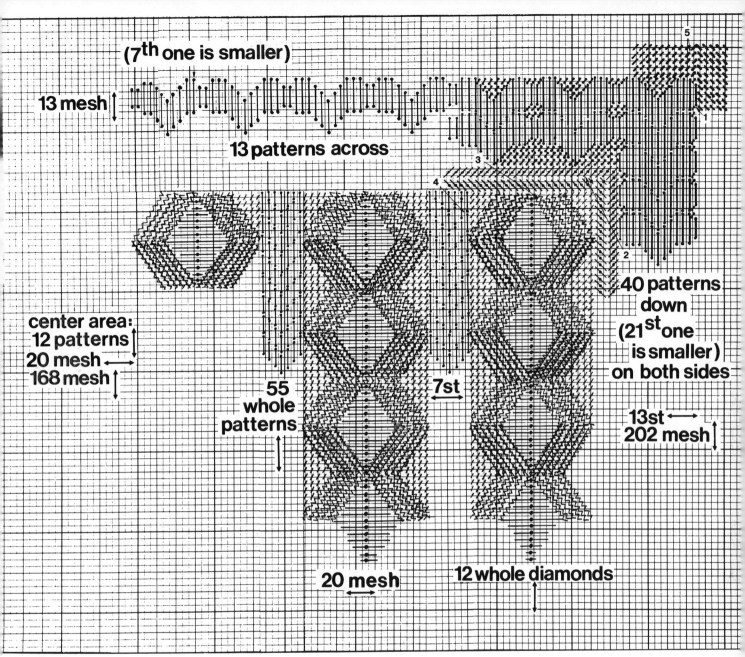

(7th one is smaller)

13 mesh ↕

13 patterns across

5

3

4

2

1

center area:
12 patterns ↕
20 mesh ⟷
168 mesh ↕

55 whole patterns ↕

7st ⟷

40 patterns down (21st one is smaller) on both sides

13st ⟷
202 mesh ↕

20 mesh ⟷

12 whole diamonds ↕

Graph *of upper right-hand portion*

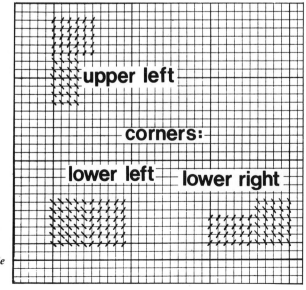

upper left

corners:

lower left   **lower right**

Right: Special corner graphs illustrating how side stitches slant inward for area (5)

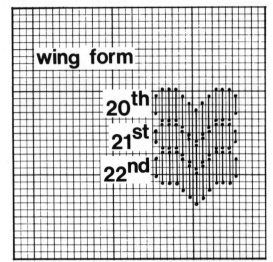

wing form

20th

21st

22nd

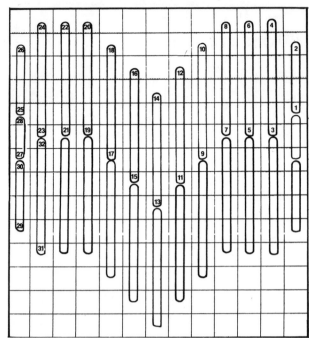

Above: Upright Gobelin stitches forming wing pattern (photo, left) for area (1). On photograph, small stitches between wing patterns have been eliminated for clarity. Above left: 21st pattern on right and left sides covers fewer mesh

Right: Upright Gobelin stitches forming chevron design (photo, below)

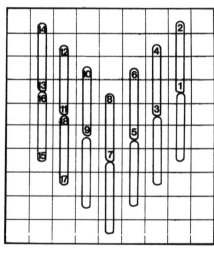

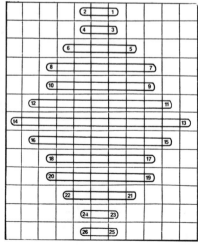

Photo and diagram (left): Gobelin stitches worked horizontally for inside of block

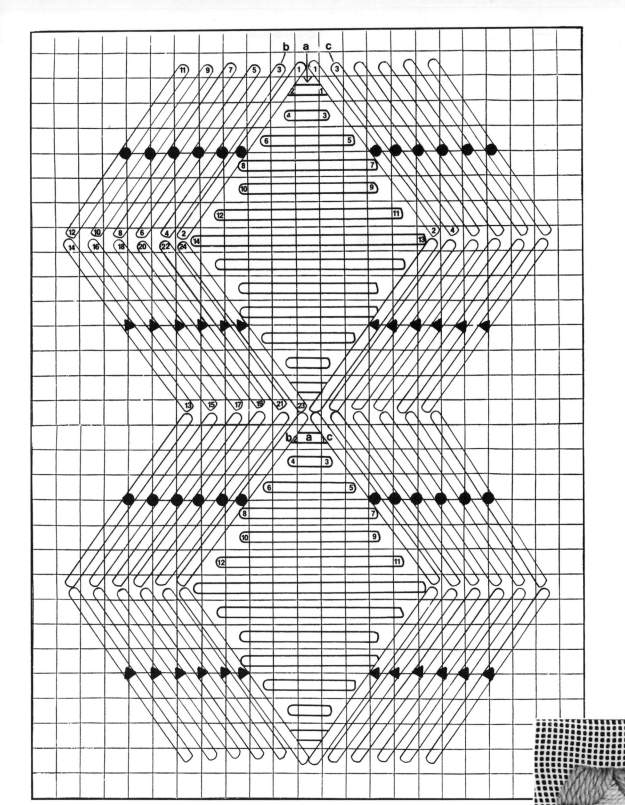

Above: Diagonal Gobelin stitches for outside of blocks and Gobelin worked horizontally for inside of blocks (photo, right); three different colors are used to form pattern

Stars and Stripes

In color, see page 47.

The pattern name suggests a simple patriotism but the colors represent the quilt maker's unique interpretation.

Work the needlepoint on a piece of 20³/₄" x 24" #13 mono interlocked canvas. Approximate size of finished needlepoint is 14³/₄" x 18".

Circled numbers indicate order in which to work areas of canvas.
Letters indicate stitches with which to work areas of canvas.
Uncircled numbers indicate colors with which to work areas of canvas.

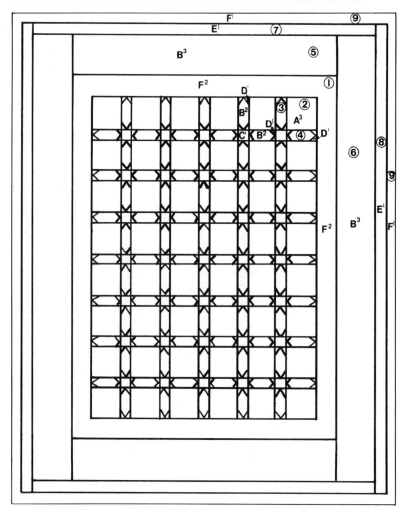

Outline

Stitches

A. diamond satin, 2-4-6-4-2 vertical pattern
B. leaf
C. Gobelin (for star)
D. Gobelin (for stripe)
E. Gobelin, vertical and horizontal patterns
F. continental or basketweave

Suggested method of working this pattern

For all stitches use the complete three-ply strand, except for the continental or basketweave which requires two plies. Count 19 mesh down and 19 mesh in from right edge of area to be worked. Begin area (1) here, working continental or basketweave to fill in approximately 3 inches across top. Then work continental or basketweave down right side for 3 inches. Start area (2) where arrow directs you on graph. Work a box of diamond satin in 2-4-6-4-2 vertical pattern. Following the graph (opposite top), the close-up graph of center design area (opposite below), and extra stitch diagrams and photographs of needlepoint stitches (overleaf), begin working a vertical stripe and a star, area (3). Continue across the top row, areas (2) and (3), alternating the boxes of diamond satin with the stripes and stars. Area (4) is a series of horizontal stripes and stars. To work horizontal patterns easily, turn the canvas so the top is to your left. Work the entire row. Complete center design area, turning canvas as necessary to make stitching easier. Complete area (1). Proceed to area (5) at top and bottom of needlepoint, and work two rows of leaf stitches (see overleaf right) horizontally across by turning the canvas on its side. Add backstitches which fill in the area after completing the rows (see overleaf right). Work leaf down right and left sides, area (6). Add backstitches. Work upright Gobelin over 4 mesh across top, area (7), and across the corresponding area on the bottom. Work area (8) on right and corresponding area on left in Gobelin, horizontal pattern. For area (9) work two rows of continental or basketweave all around entire design.

Colors	Craft Persian yarn color #	# of 32" strands used
1. pink	5	55
2. celadon	114	71
3. navy	95	101

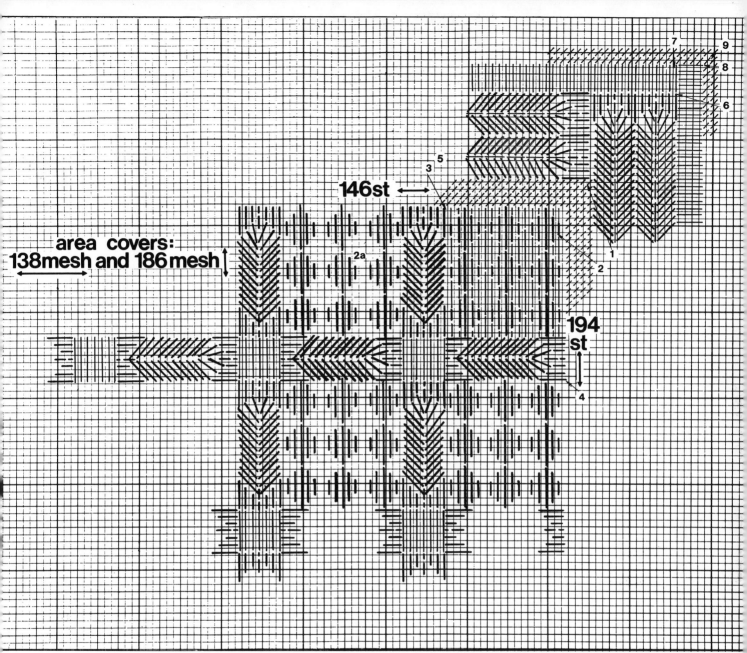

area covers:
138mesh and 186mesh

146st →

194 st

Graph *of upper right-hand portion*

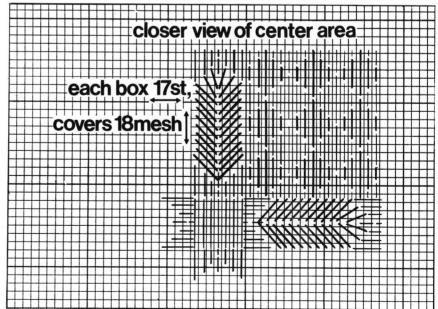

closer view of center area

each box 17st, →

covers 18mesh ↕

Right: Close-up view of part of center design area with diamond satin, 2-4-6-4-2 vertical pattern; Gobelin for star; Gobelin stitches for beginning and end of stripe; leaf

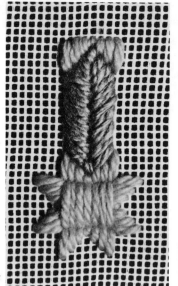

*Photo and diagram (right):
Gobelin for beginning and end
of a stripe; leaf; upright Gobelin
for star*

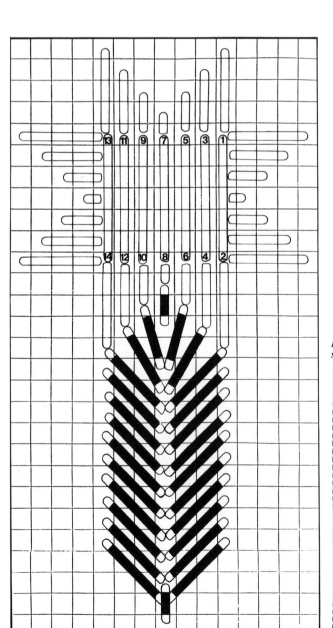

*Left: Gobelin for star; leaf
stitch for stripe (photo, below)*

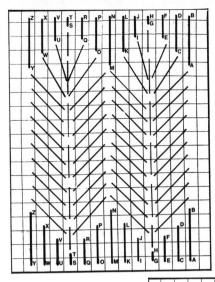

Left: Two rows of leaf with backstitches and Gobelin for beginning and end of a stripe

Above: Gobelin for a star (photo, right)

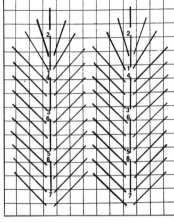

Right: Two rows of leaf with backstitches

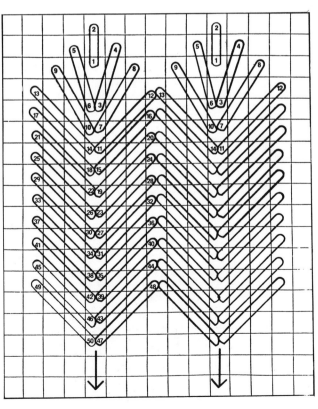

Left: Two rows of leaf (photo, below)

119

Baskets or Cake Stand

In color, see page 47.

Cranberry, strawberry, and turquoise give the needlepoint its glowing appearance; beige softens the overall effect.

Work needlepoint on a piece of 22³/₄″ x 22¹/₂″ #13 mono interlocked canvas. Approximate size of finished piece is 16³/₄″ x 16¹/₂″.

Circled numbers indicate order in which to work areas of canvas.
Letters indicate stitches with which to work areas of canvas.
Uncircled numbers indicate colors with which to work areas of canvas.

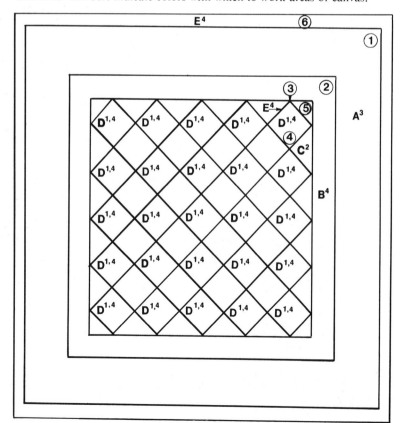

Outline

Stitches

A. diamond satin, 2-4-6-4-2 vertical pattern
B. double brick
C. Parisian
D. Gobelin, vertical and horizontal patterns, plus continental
E. continental

Suggested method of working this pattern

For all stitches use the complete three-ply strand except for the continental which requires two plies. Area (1) is worked in diamond satin, 2-4-6-4-2 vertical pattern. Beginning in upper right corner, fill in area (1) across the top for 4 inches and then down right side for another 4 inches. Next move to area (2) and use the double brick (below and opposite below left). Work it across top for 3 inches and down right side for 3 inches. You can now begin the center design area. Following the graph (opposite above) and outline (left below), work the diamonds and half-diamonds. First work area (3), the outline of a diamond, in cranberry continental stitches. Inside the diamond work the basket, area (4), in pink beige Gobelin stitches, both vertically and horizontally. Fill in remaining areas of diamond with continental in cranberry (opposite below right). Now work a quarter-diamond in Parisian in turquoise, area (5). Work across the top of center design area, using continental where outline is marked E^4; the basket pattern and continental where outline is marked $D^{1,4}$; and Parisian, C^2, where diamonds, half-diamonds, and quarter-diamonds are blank. Complete center design in this manner. Complete areas (2) and (1) on all four sides. Move to area (6) and work two rows of continental on all sides.

Colors	Craft Persian yarn color #	# of 32″ strands used
1. pink beige	139	21
2. turquoise	782	74
3. strawberry	10	66
4. cranberry	9	50

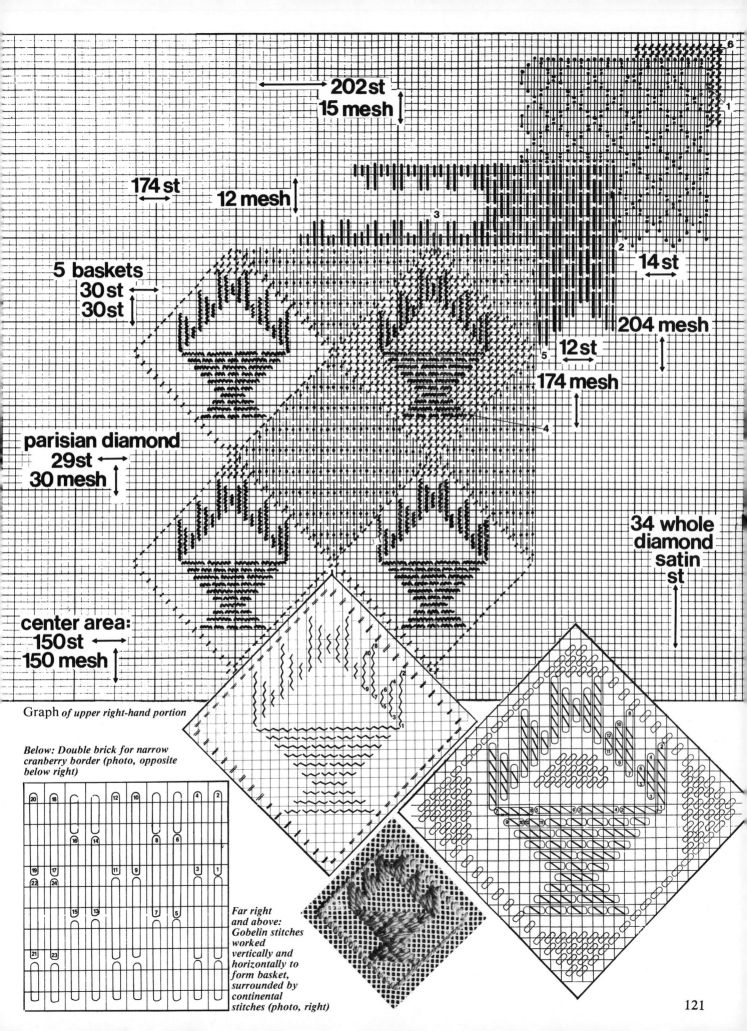

202 st
15 mesh

174 st
12 mesh

5 baskets
30 st
30 st

parisian diamond
29 st
30 mesh

center area:
150 st
150 mesh

14 st

204 mesh

12 st
174 mesh

34 whole diamond satin st

Graph *of upper right-hand portion*

Below: Double brick for narrow cranberry border (photo, opposite below right)

Far right and above: Gobelin stitches worked vertically and horizontally to form basket, surrounded by continental stitches (photo, right)

121

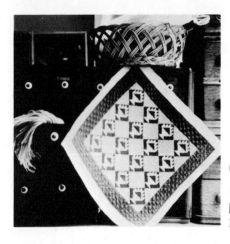

Baskets or Cake Stand

In color, see page 47.

Another Basket quilt, but the use of different colors— pink, green, turquoise— gives it a very different air.

Work needlepoint on a piece of 18½″ x 18½″ #12 mono interlocked canvas. Approximate size of finished piece is 12½″ x 12½″.

Circled numbers indicate order in which to work areas of canvas.
Letters indicate stitches with which to work areas of canvas.
Uncircled numbers indicate colors with which to work areas of canvas.

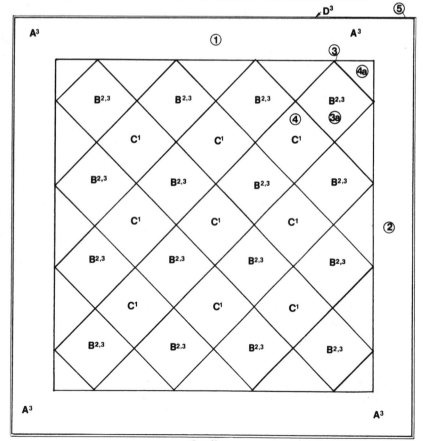

Outline

Stitches

A. checkerboard (continental and Scotch)
B. Gobelin, vertical and horizontal patterns, plus continental
C. Parisian
D. continental

Suggested method of working this pattern

For all stitches use the complete three-ply strand except for the continental which requires two plies. Begin this needlepoint in area (1) at the top right-hand corner. Use the checkerboard stitch, which consists of continental and Scotch (opposite above left). Work it across top. There will be a total of 19 squares of continental and 19 squares of Scotch in each row and a total of four rows. Work each square separately. Do not carry yarn across the back of canvas because this distorts canvas. Turning canvas upside down for alternate rows further minimizes canvas distortion. Area (2) is continuation of this pattern down right side. Work it for 5 inches. Start area (3) where arrow directs. First outline diamond with continental stitches according to graph (opposite above right) in loden. Fill it in with a basket made of Gobelin in pink and surrounded by continental in loden (see diagrams, opposite below right). Note: Continental stitches around basket are not shown on graph so basket can stand out. Work part of a diamond, area (4a), and then a whole diamond, area (4), in turquoise Parisian stitches (diagram, opposite below left). Complete entire center design according to outline (left). Complete area (2) down right side, down left side, across bottom. Work area (5), two rows of continental all around.

Colors	Craft Persian yarn color #	# of 32″ strands used
1. pale turquoise	81	48
2. pale pink	13	29
3. loden	64	125

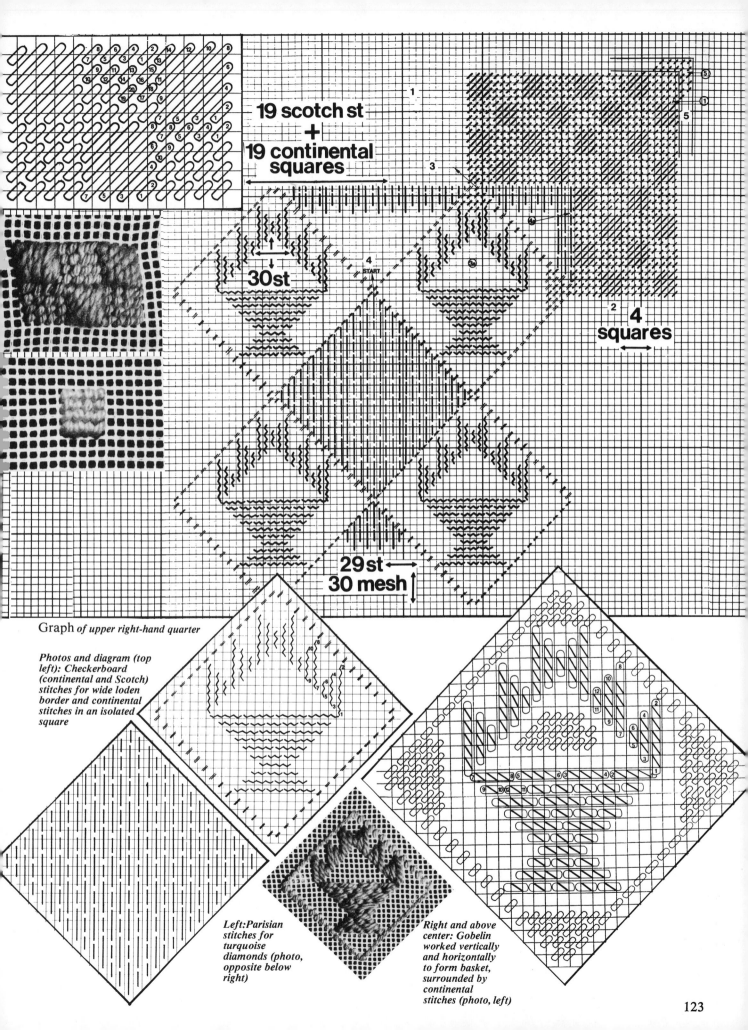

19 scotch st
+
19 continental
squares

30st

29 st
30 mesh

1

3

2

4 squares

4
START

5

Graph *of upper right-hand quarter*

Photos and diagram (top left): Checkerboard (continental and Scotch) stitches for wide loden border and continental stitches in an isolated square

Left: Parisian stitches for turquoise diamonds (photo, opposite below right)

Right and above center: Gobelin worked vertically and horizontally to form basket, surrounded by continental stitches (photo, left)

Jake Mast

In color, see page 48.

Named for its maker, Jake Mast, this quilt is a rare example of one made by an Amish man.

Work needlepoint on a piece of 18″ x 18⅞″ #13 mono interlocked canvas. Approximate size of finished needlepoint is 12″ x 12⅞″.

Circled numbers indicate order in which to work areas of canvas. Letters indicate stitches with which to work areas of canvas. For colors, see special color chart (overleaf right).

Outline

Stitches

A. double leviathan
B. Gobelin, vertical and horizontal patterns (over 4 mesh)
C. stem
D. Gobelin, vertical and horizontal patterns (over 3 mesh)
E. Gobelin (for cone border)
F. continental or basketweave

Suggested method of working this pattern

For all stitches use the complete three-ply strand, except for the continental or basketweave which requires two plies. Starting at area (1), work double leviathans in diagonal lines that crisscross in the center design area (see outline, left below, and graph, opposite top). Use a loose tension when working double leviathan to add extra height to the stitch. Work Gobelin in area (2), boxes between double leviathan chains. The Gobelin stitches are worked vertically and horizontally over 4 mesh (see stitch diagram, overleaf left). Note: There are 2 stitches in the same space at beginning and end of each row of Gobelin stitches. Consult color chart (overleaf right) for correct colors. For area (3) use the stem stitch. Work it down right side first and clockwise around center design. To work cone border, area (4), again consult the color chart. Blank spaces indicate use of white. Work this area in Gobelin stitches that cover different numbers of mesh (see graph, opposite top). Use a loose tension to prevent canvas from showing. For corners consult special graphs (opposite below). For area (5) work Gobelin over 3 mesh: upright stitches on top and bottom and horizontal stitches at sides. To complete design, work two rows of continental or basketweave in area (6).

Colors	Craft Persian yarn color #	# of 32″ strands used
1. medium mauve	3	6
2. pale pink	13	30
3. burgundy	17	10
4. peach	23	8
5. light orange	31	6
6. maize	44	6
7. old bronze	47	6
8. antique bronze	54	9
9. army green	55	9
10. leaf green	56	6
11. peacock blue	79	12
12. pale blue	83	9
13. sea blue	84	16

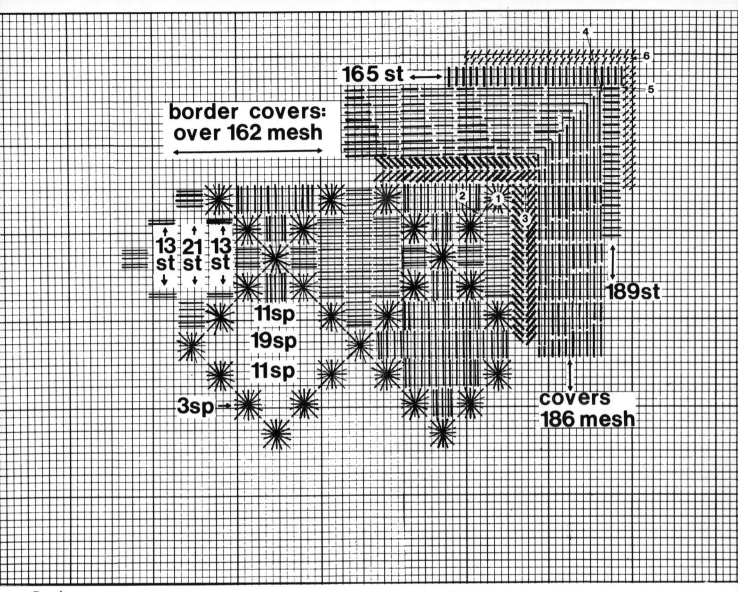

165 st ⟷

**border covers:
over 162 mesh**

13 st **21 st** **13 st**

11sp

19sp

11sp

3sp →

189st

**covers
186 mesh**

Graph *of upper right-hand corner*

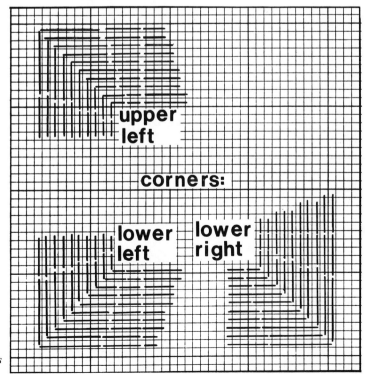

**upper
left**

corners:

**lower
left**

**lower
right**

*Right: Gobelin in corners
of cone border pattern*

14. blue	85	9
15. blueberry	86	17
16. light violet	91	6
17. navy	95	13
18. black	96	15
19. blue gray	97	15
20. pewter	98	11
21. light gray	99	9
22. pale gray	100	6
23. white	101	99
24. ecru	103	6
25. wheat	104	6
26. coffee	105	8
27. caramel	108	7
28. dark olive	112	8
29. olive	113	9
30. celadon	114	15
31. French blue	116	9
32. storm blue	117	7
33. sky blue	118	7
34. camel	121	6
35. light plum	126	7
36. rose pink	130	8
37. pale rose	131	6
38. med. slate blue	134	7
39. light slate blue	135	6

Below: Gobelin over 4 mesh both vertically and horizontally and double leviathan for center design area (photo, left)

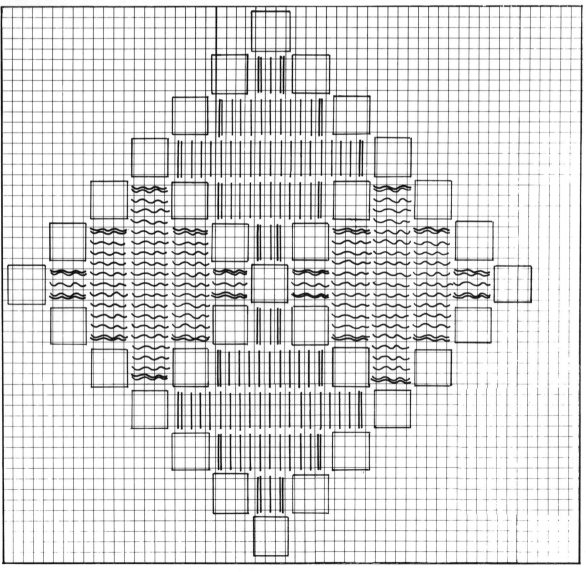

Color Chart *for Jake Mast quilt*
Uncircled numbers indicate colors with which to work areas of canvas.
Blank spaces indicate use of white.

Additional stitches

The additional stitches here and on the next three pages offer possibilities for small areas, narrow and wide borders, and backgrounds other than those already specified. Work these stitches in the same manner you worked the others. Note the direction of each stitch (whether it runs horizontally, vertically, diagonally), the number of mesh it covers, the order of steps that form it (indicated by the numbers). When used in multiples, many of these stitches produce designs that are remarkably similar to quilting patterns. Use these stitches if you independently translate other quilts into needlepoint, or to vary ours. Practice stitches that are unfamiliar to you, and remember to include compensating stitches when you even off an area or edge.

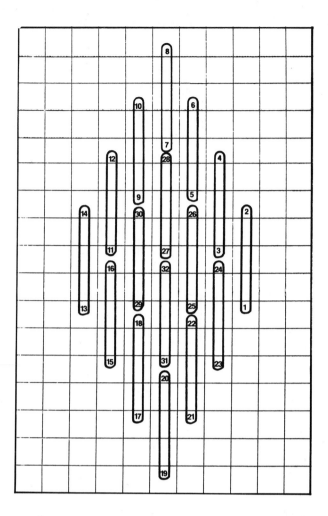

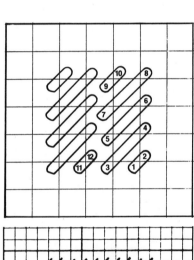

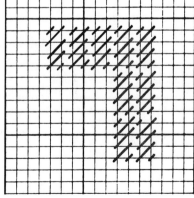

Upright cashmere

Top: With this diagonally worked stitch (numbers 1 through 10), which covers varying numbers of mesh, you create a narrow rectangle. Use a loose tension when stitching because it has a tendency to distort the canvas. Inverting the canvas for alternate rows helps. You can use this stitch for a narrow border (above) or to fill a background.

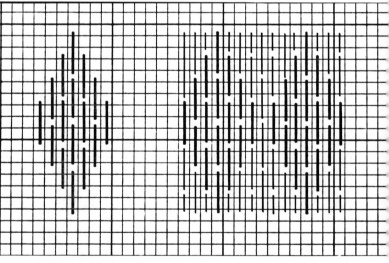

Florentine diamond

Top and above left: Every upright Gobelin stitch in this long, narrow diamond covers 4 mesh. To use the Florentine diamond in a background, surround the diamond with more upright Gobelin stitches in another color (above right) or with continental stitches. You can also work the diamond horizontally.

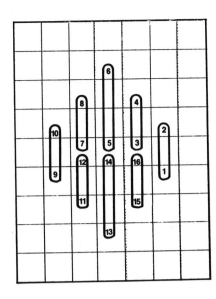

Small diamond

Left: The outline of the small diamond is similar to that of the diamond satin, 2-4-6-4-2 vertical pattern (see stitch glossary, page 30). In both patterns the outside stitches cover 2 mesh. Here, however, the inner stitches are divided into two halves. You can surround this small diamond with upright Gobelin stitches over 3 mesh plus compensating stitches (below left) or upright Gobelin over 4 mesh plus compensating stitches (below right).

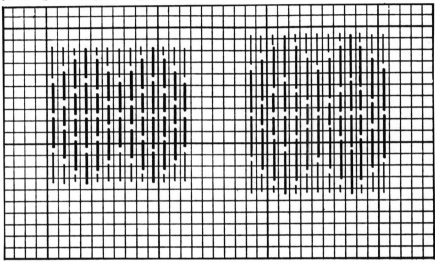

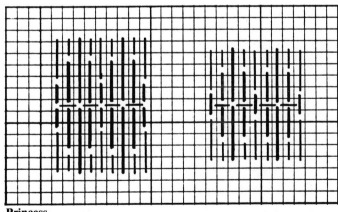

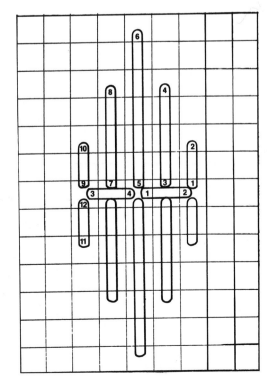

Princess

Left: Here is a pattern that combines vertical and horizontal stitches. There are upright Gobelin stitches over varying numbers of threads at top and bottom, and horizontal stitches over 2 mesh at the center. First work the top; then the bottom, a mirror image of the top; and finally the center. Surround stitches with more upright Gobelin (above left). For a variation work just one upright Gobelin over 2 mesh at each side and shorten each inner stitch by 1 mesh (above right).

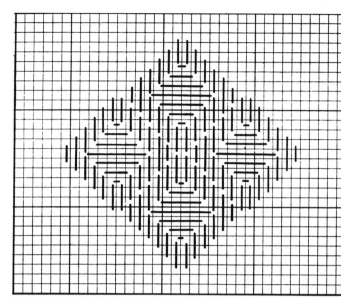

Diamond satin variations

Here are three variations of the 2-4-6-8-6-4-2 diamond satin. In the first example (left) upright Gobelin stitches surround diamond satins to yield the unusual effect of diamonds within diamonds, forming one large diamond. You can work all the stitches in one color or try using one color for the inner diamonds and a second color for surrounding areas. You can also work the diamond satin with a backstitch between diamonds (below left). Use compensating half-diamonds at top, bottom, and sides (below center). Work the backstitches after you have completed the diamonds. Or try surrounding the diamonds with upright Gobelin stitches over 4 mesh (below right). Finish with compensating stitches.

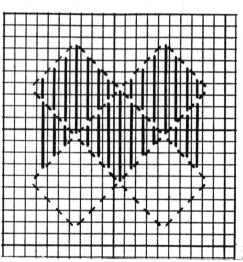

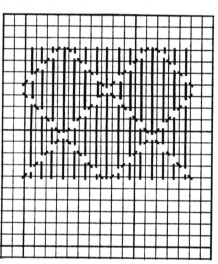

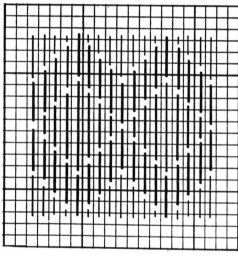

Milanese

The Milanese stitch (right) is very effective for a large border or background (far right) because the length of the stitches increases within each pattern unit (numbers 1 through 8). Be sure to use a loose tension since some of the stitches must cover many mesh. Work from bottom to top of canvas, then from top to bottom. If you work this stitch for a large background, try using different shades of one color each time you change stitching direction.

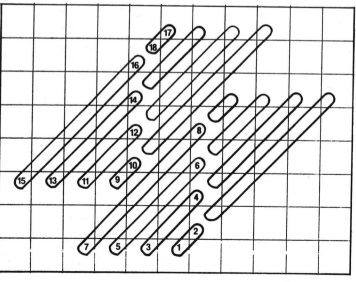

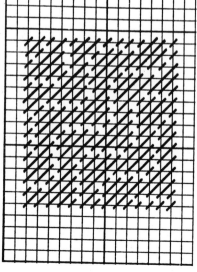

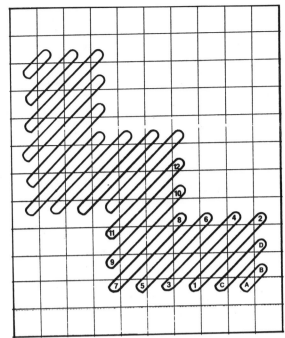

Byzantine

The stitches with numbers are the basis of this zigzag pattern (left); the stitches with letters are compensating stitches. In this example each diagonally worked stitch covers 3 mesh, but you can vary the length of the stitches and the number of stitches between each step to suit your particular project. This stitch is especially appropriate as a border or background (left below), since it can be worked fairly quickly.

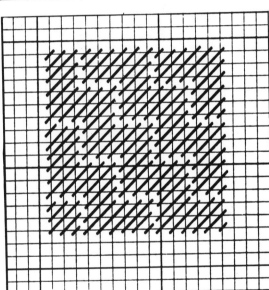

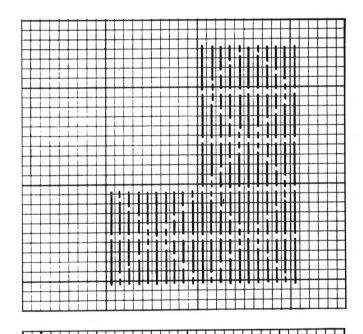

Small triangles

These stitches form a pattern reminiscent of the pieced quilt, Triangles. Worked as a border (above right), these small triangles would look handsome all in one color or in a rainbow of shades (as in Railroad Crossing on pages 44–45). Another border (right) varies slightly from the border above. In it Gobelin stitches are worked horizontally and the number of mesh covered is varied slightly.

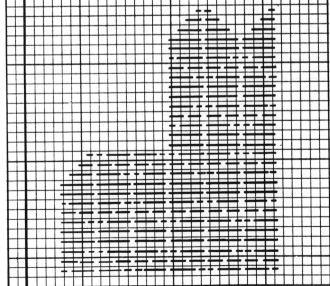

Alphabets

Although Amish quilt makers rarely signed their designs, you may want to sign and date your own work. The three alphabets and two sets of numerals we show are all worked in continental stitch.

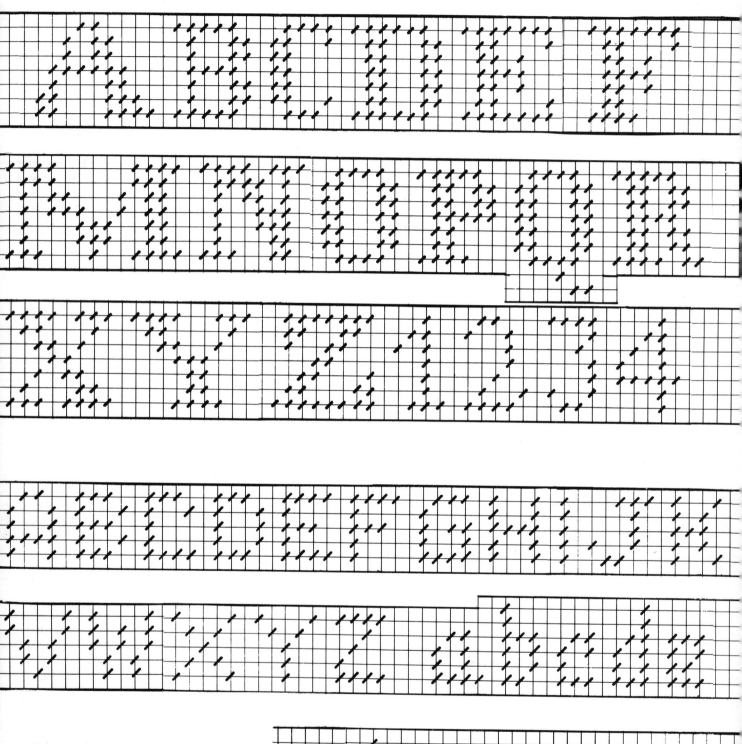

Simple linear letters

If you are needlepointing a monogram, you can carry your thread across from one letter to the next. But if you needlepoint a long name or inscription, end off a piece of yarn after you have worked a few letters.

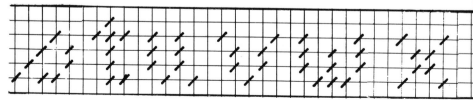

Double-edged bold style

There are many styles of alphabets to choose from. If you want the monogram to be bold and forthright, select an alphabet such as this one (above)

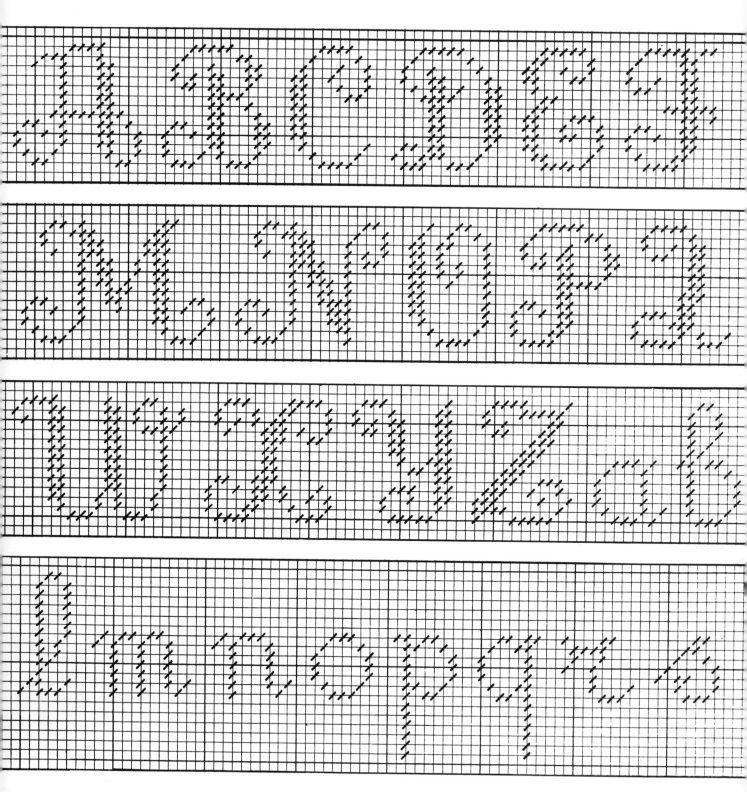

Old-fashioned script

Although ornate, the alphabet and accompanying set of numbers are easy to work. Always count how many mesh the letters and numbers cover to be sure they fit into the area where you plan to work them. Be sure also to space letters and numerals evenly.

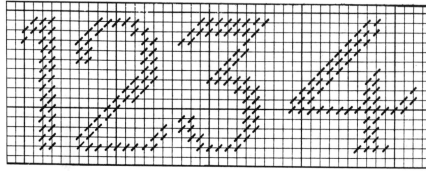

134

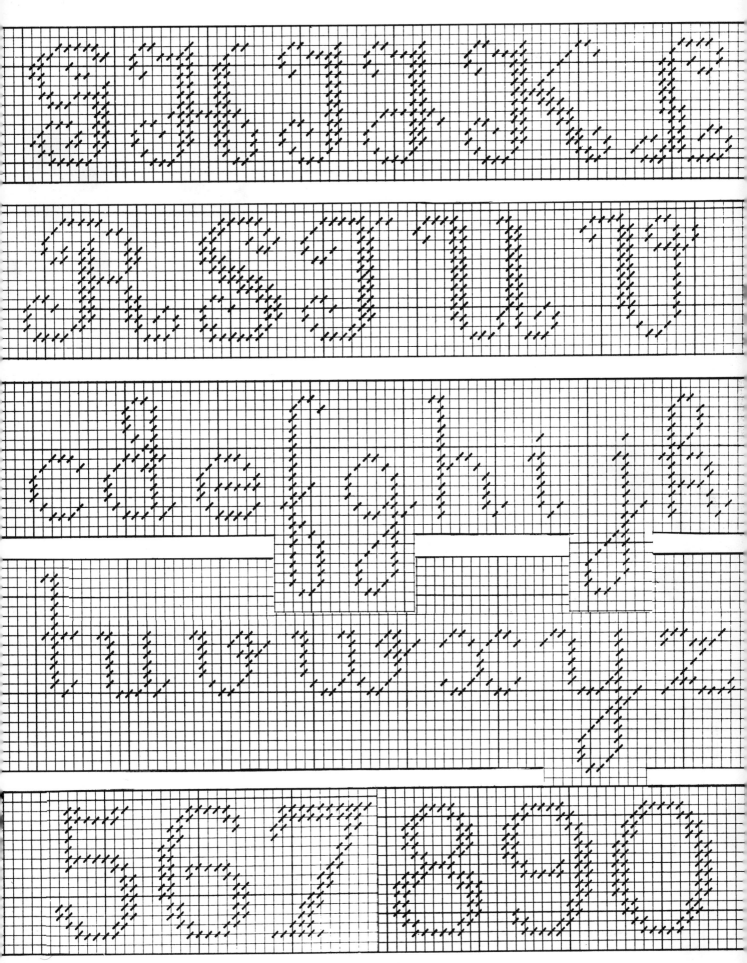

135

Monograms

After you have mastered the stitching of letters and numerals (previous pages), you can incorporate them into specific projects. In many works of art, including samplers and paintings such as Robert Indiana's famous *Love*, letters and numerals are actually the basis of the design. In these Amish needlepoints, however, the initials and date should be of minimal importance. Therefore choose a style and size of lettering that will not compete with your particular Amish choice.

Discreet signature

Near the bottom of one of the center stripes in the Bars needlepoint (above) work your initials and the date you completed it (below). If you are presenting this to a friend, add those initials in another bar.

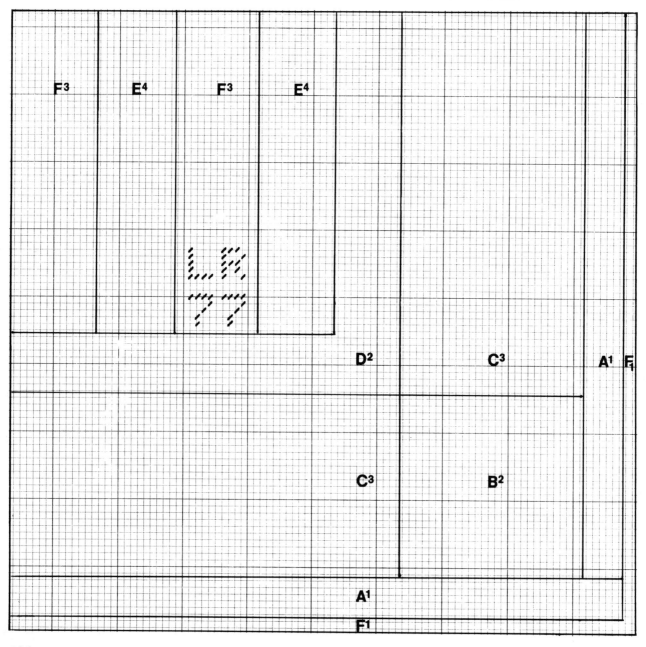

Center stage

If you have a special reason to emphasize the maker and date, you can eliminate some of the baskets at the center of the Baskets needlepoint (above) and work the monogram and the year there (below and right). The design will then depart from the Amish and become somewhat reminiscent of friendship quilts, which included the signatures and dates of those who contributed squares. We recommend working initials and date in the same pink beige used for the baskets.

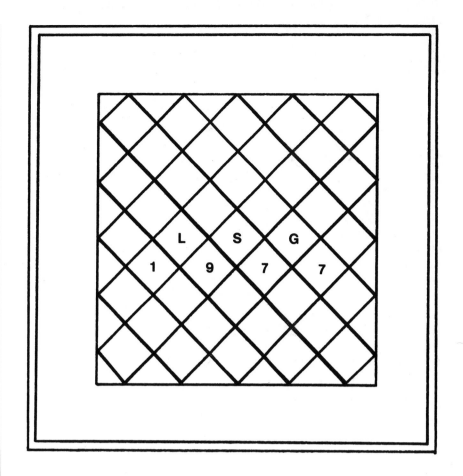

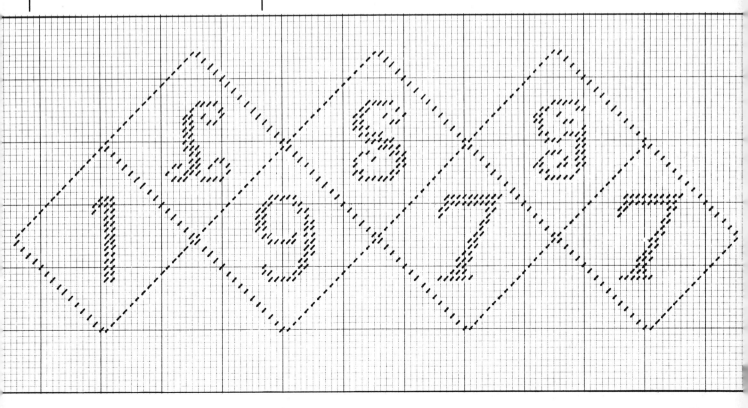

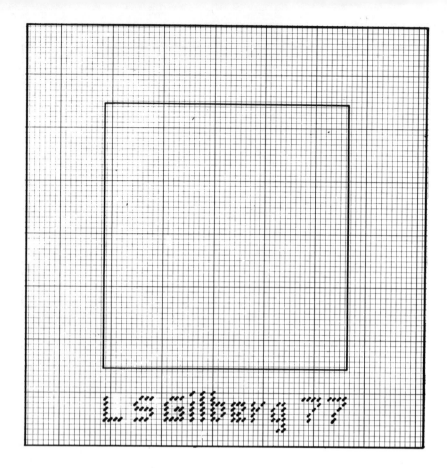

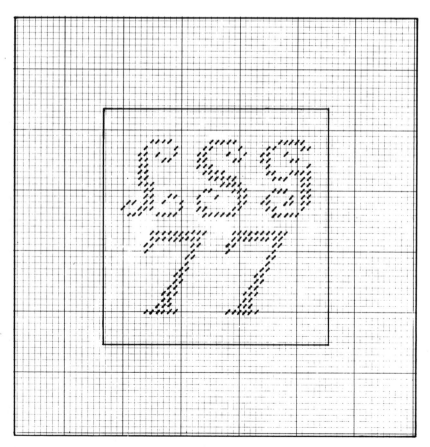

Front or back monogram

The Sunshine and Shadow needlepoint (above) inspired two very different methods of personalizing. If you want to turn your needlepoint into a picture, work a separate rectangle with your name and date. Have a framer insert this needlepoint in a window in the mat (left) when design is framed. If you prefer the needlepoint as a pillow and wish to work a complete backing piece, take a piece of canvas the same size as your Amish design and work a center square with monogram and date (below left). Surround this square with stitches in any pattern. This design will become the back of your pillow.

Signed soft tapestry

If you want to work the Railroad Crossing (above) as a signed soft tapestry, you might include an extra area where you will sign your name and date (detail right) plus the regular 3 inches of blank canvas on every side. The monogrammed border will serve as a needlepointed frame for the Amish design. When the work is blocked, have a strip of canvas sewn on the back so you can slip a curtain rod through and hang the needlepoint picture on the wall.

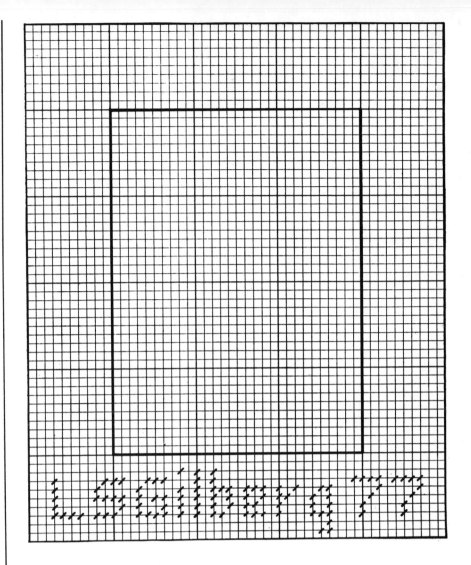

Border idea

In the narrow 5-mesh-high green frame around the center design of Lone Star (above), you can subtly work your initials and the date. Use continental stitches for the alphabet and date (right) and use the color navy, which repeats the background of the star. Many designs in this book lend themselves to such a signature.

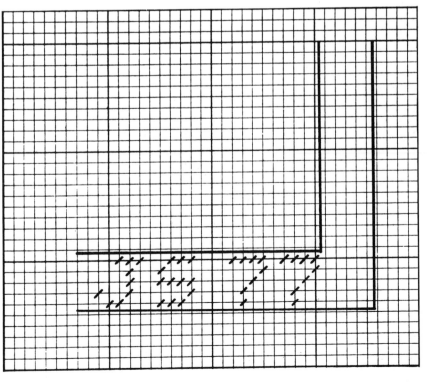

Yarn Chart

How to find the corresponding colors of Persian yarn in other types of thread

This chart enables you to work your own interpretations of our Amish designs. For example, you may like the Baby's Block Variation pattern (page 46 in color) but you may prefer to use Veloura velvet yarn instead of the Persian yarn we used. To identify the corresponding Veloura colors, find each Persian yarn color number used in that design in the left-hand column marked *Craft Persian yarn color #* and move across to the column marked *Veloura*. To see the difference the yarn makes, look at Railroad Crossing in Persian yarn (pages 44–45 in color) and Railroad Crossing in Veloura (pages 40–41 in color). Because some of the special yarns and threads are not available in as wide a color range as Persian yarns are, you may have to make a substitution occasionally. We made substitutions when we compiled this list, and we suggest that you consult the color photographs of the needlepoints before purchasing your yarns. It would, in fact, be helpful if you take the book with you when purchasing your yarns.

Craft Persian yarn color #	Veloura Velvet yarn color #	Craft yarn's Craftacryl rug yarn color #	Paternayan's Pat rug yarn color #	Brunswick precut acrylic rug yarn color #	Brunswick precut wool rug yarn color #	D.M.C. pearl cotton #1 color #	D.M.C. pearl cotton #3 color #	D.M.C. embroidery thread color #
3	425	142	253	130	30	818		
4	406					776	776	604
5		141	831			776	605	605
6			279	132	32		603	603
7		140	239	128	28	210	601	601
9	403		209	134	34	309	718	718
10			219	128	28	309	498	498
11	404	143	251	132	32		892	892
12			253	133	33	776	894	894
13	406	117	831	163	63	818	818	818
16	404	137	241	135	35	309	309	309
17		136	233	134	34	815	815	815
18	405	116	818	156	56	321	321	321
21	406		878	163	63	776	776	776
22	406		018	107	7	819	948	948
23		173	853	107	7	945	353	353
24		174	852	110	10		758	758
25		116	852	109	9		947	947
26		135	843	109	9	606	606	606
27			242	135	35	321	321	321
28		134	843	110	10		351	351
31	415	120	444	157	57	742	742	742
32	411		452			744	945	945
356	416	119	225	137	37		976	976
37	403		267	137	37		356	356
38	428	153	410	154	54		975	975
408	413		421	113	13	783	783	783
44	412		453	162	62	744	744	744
45	413		445	162	62	725	725	725
46	413	118	433	112	12	783	783	783
47			124	106	6		730	730
486	413		421	116	16		729	729
54	414	122	521	168	68		732	732
55	408		919	140	40	470	937	937
56	407		545	145	45	907	471	471
64	431	179	505	141	41	3345	3345	3345
65	410	110	559	142	42	911	702	702
66	409	178	579	146	46	905	703	703
70	409	108	536	146	46	955	955	955
73	410		526	142	42	911	909	909
74	431	111	524	141	41	911	911	911
782	432	113	728	120	20		995	995
79	423	114	316	121	21	336	336	336
81	421	115	738	122	22		807	807
824	420		759	158	58		800	800
83	429	169	749	171	71	799	799	799

Craft Persian yarn color #	Veloura Velvet yarn color #	Craft yarn's Craftacryl rug yarn color #	Paternayan's Pat rug yarn color #	Brunswick precut acrylic rug yarn color #	Brunswick precut wool rug yarn color #	D.M.C. pearl cotton #1 color #	D.M.C. pearl cotton #3 color #	D.M.C. embroidery thread color #
84	429	104	739	172	72	798	798	798
85	423		729	173	73	797	797	797
855	423	112	723	173	73	797	797	797
86	423	102	731	118	18	796	796	796
87	426	103	662	127	27			793
89	425		682					794
91	425		618				210	210
93	426	139	632				208	208
94	426	138	622				552	552
95	424	101	305	117	17	823	823	823
96	402	124	050	150	50	310	310	310
97			182	103	3	413	413	413
98	432		184	101	1	414	414	414
99	432	148	186	102	2	415	415	415
100			011	151	51	762	762	762
101	401	132	005	149	49	SNOW WHITE	SNOW WHITE	SNOW WHITE
102	417	147	020	151	51	712	712	712
103	411		492	152	52	822	822	822
104			466	155	55	842	738	738
105	419	155	145	106	6	801	801	801
106	419	155	144	104	4	898	898	898
108	427	161	172	108	8	433	434	434
112		151	527			3345	3345	3345
113		162	542			320	320	320
114		150	566			368	368	368
115		165	592			955	504	504
116	423	171	334	160	60	336	930	930
117	429	170	385	159	59	932	932	932
118	422	105	395	158	58	827	827	827
121	427	126	194	153	53	712	712	712
122	418		496	155	55	644	644	644
124			610	125	25		552	552
125	426		612	126	26		552	550
126			615	131	31		208	208
128	403	146	236	134	34	3685	3685	3685
129		145	250	132	32		309	309
130	405	167	289	164	64		899	899
131	404	166	254	163	63	776	776	776
132			365	161	61	336	336	336
133		172	334	160	60	332	332	332
134			385	159	59	322	322	322
135	421	170	182	101	1		322	322
136	421		395	158	58	827	828	828
139	418	152	133	167	67	842	842	842
140	417		143			822	822	822

Bibliography

Needlepoint books for further study:

Borssuck, B. *97 Needlepoint Alphabets.* New York: Arco Publishing Co., Inc., 1975.

Bucher, Jo. *Complete Guide to Creative Needlepoint.* Des Moines: Creative Home Library, 1973.

Christensen, Jo Ippolito. *The Needlepoint Book.* Englewood Cliffs, N.J.: Prentice-Hall, Inc., 1976.

Davis, Mary Kay, and Giammattei, Helen. *Needlepoint from America's Great Quilt Designs.* New York: Workman Publishing Co., 1974.

De Dillmont, Therese. *Encyclopedia of Needlework.* Mulhouse, France: Editions Th. De Dillmont, 1975.

Gartner, Louis J., Jr. *More Needlepoint Design.* New York: William Morrow & Co., 1975.

Gartner, Louis J., Jr. *Needlepoint Design.* New York: William Morrow & Co., 1970.

Hanley, Hope. *Needlepoint,* rev. ed. New York: Charles Scribner's Sons, 1975.

Rome, Carol C., and Devlin, Georgia F. *A New Look at Needlepoint: The Complete Guide to Canvas Embroidery with 80 Different Stitches.* New York: Crown Publishers, Inc., 1972.

Books relating to the Amish and their quilts:

Bishop, Robert. *New Discoveries in American Quilts.* New York: E. P. Dutton & Co., 1975.

Bishop, Robert, and Safanda, Elizabeth. *A Gallery of Amish Quilts.* New York: E. P. Dutton & Co., 1976.

Brand, Millen. *Fields of Peace.* New York: E. P. Dutton & Co., 1973.

Haders, Phyllis. *Sunshine and Shadow: The Amish and Their Quilts.* New York: The Main Street Press, 1976.

Holstein, Jonathan. *American Pieced Quilts.* New York: The Viking Press, Inc., 1972.

Holstein, Jonathan. *The Pieced Quilt.* Greenwich, Conn.: New York Graphic Society, 1973.

Hostetler, John A. *Amish Society.* Baltimore: Johns Hopkins University Press, 1968.

Johnson, Marilynn Bordes. *Twelve Great Quilts from the American Wing.* New York: Metropolitan Museum of Art, 1974.

Lipman, Jean, and Winchester, Alice. *The Flowering of American Folk Art, 1776–1876.* New York: The Viking Press, Inc., 1974.

Orlofsky, Patsy, and Orlofsky, Myron. *Quilts in America.* New York: McGraw-Hill Book Co., 1974.

Safford, Carleton L., and Bishop, Robert. *America's Quilts and Coverlets.* New York: E. P. Dutton & Co., 1972.

Other quilt books of interest:

Carlisle, Lilian Baker. *Pieced Work and Appliqué Quilts at Shelburne Museum.* Museum Pamphlet Series, no. 2. Shelburne, Vt.: Shelburne Museum, 1957.

Chesley, Jean Rusch. *American Pictorial Quilts.* Poughkeepsie: Vassar College Art Gallery, 1975.

Colby, Averil. *Patchwork Quilts.* New York: Charles Scribner's Sons, 1965.

Dunton, William Rush, Jr. *Old Quilts.* Maryland: By the author, 1946.

Finley, Ruth E. *Old Patchwork Quilts and the Women Who Made Them.* Newton Centre, Mass.: Charles T. Branford Co., 1971.

Hinson, Dolores A. *Quilting Manual.* New York: Hearthside Press, 1970.

Suppliers

Suppliers of our canvases and yarns:

Brunswick Yarn Company
230 Fifth Avenue, New York, New York 10001
Brunswick precut wool rug yarn packs, Brunswick #3 ½ rug canvas

Craft Yarns of Rhode Island, Inc.
Main Street, P.O. Box 151, Harrisville, Rhode Island 02830
Craft Persian yarn, Craftacryl rug yarn

D.M.C. Corporation
107 Trumbull Street, Elizabeth, New Jersey 07206
D.M.C. pearl cotton #1 and #3

Howard Needlepoint Supply, Inc.
919 Third Avenue, New York, New York 10022
#4 leno polyester interlocking canvas

Idle Hands
82-04 Lefferts Boulevard, Kew Gardens, New York 11415
Veloura velvet yarn

Mark Distributors
20825 Prairie Street, Chatsworth, California 91311
#7 interlocking needlepoint and rug canvas

Paternayan Brothers, Inc.
312 East 95th Street, New York, New York 10028
Pat rug yarn, Pat shag rug yarn, #6 rug canvas

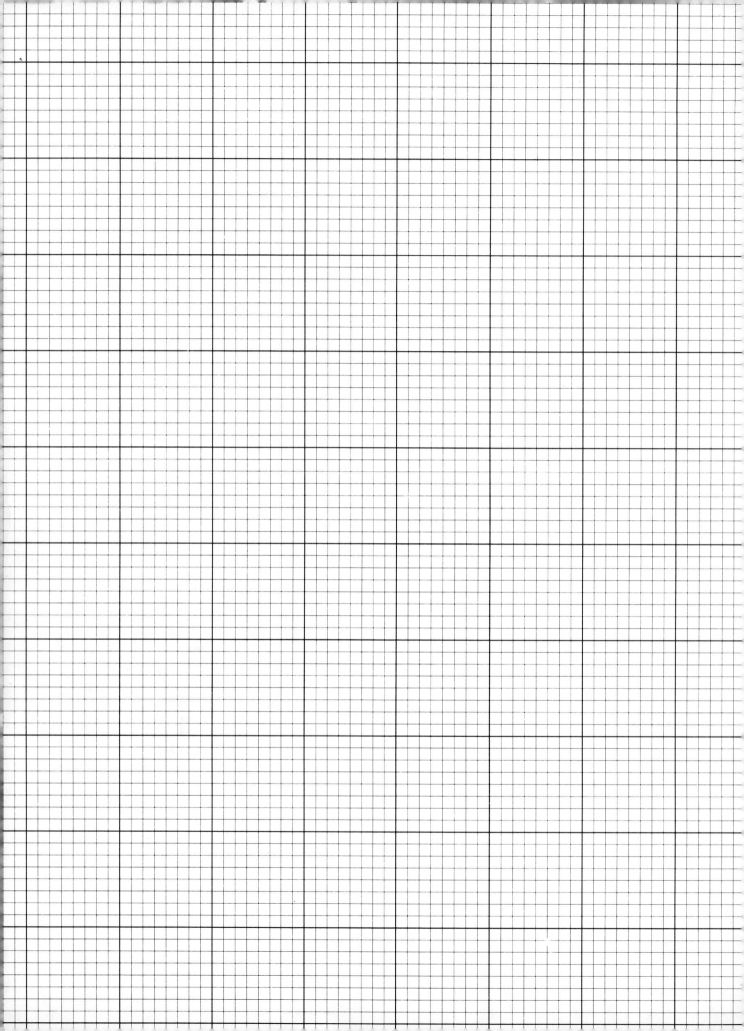